THIS BOOK BELONGS TO

_____

_____

START DATE _____ / _____ / _____

EXECUTIVE

**FOUNDER /
CHIEF EXECUTIVE OFFICER**
Raechel Myers

**CO-FOUNDER /
CHIEF CONTENT OFFICER**
Amanda Bible Williams

CHIEF OPERATING OFFICER
Ryan Myers

EXECUTIVE ASSISTANT
Catherine Cromer

EDITORIAL

CONTENT DIRECTOR
John Greco, MDiv

MANAGING EDITOR
Jessica Lamb

**PROJECT MANAGER,
KIDS READ TRUTH**
Melanie Rainer, MATS

CONTENT EDITOR
Kara Gause

ASSOCIATE EDITORS
Bailey Gillespie
Ellen Taylor

CREATIVE

CREATIVE DIRECTOR
Jeremy Mitchell

LEAD DESIGNER
Kelsea Allen

ARTIST IN RESIDENCE
Emily Knapp

DESIGNERS
Abbey Benson
Davis DeLisi

MARKETING

MARKETING DIRECTOR
Casey Campbell

MARKETING MANAGER
Katie Matuska

SOCIAL MEDIA STRATEGIST
Ansley Rushing

CHURCH PARTNERSHIP SPECIALIST
Kamiren Passavanti

COMMUNITY SUPPORT SPECIALIST
Margot Williams

SHIPPING & LOGISTICS

LOGISTICS MANAGER
Lauren Gloyne

SHIPPING MANAGER
Sydney Bess

FULFILLMENT COORDINATOR
Katy McKnight

FULFILLMENT SPECIALISTS
Sam Campos
Julia Rogers

SUBSCRIPTION INQUIRIES
churches@shereadstruth.com

CONTRIBUTORS

Amanda Barnhart, recipes
Alyssa Bustin, photography
(cover, 60, 192, 244, 260)
Rebecca Faires
Russ Ramsey

COLOPHON

This book was printed offset in Nashville, Tennessee, on 60# Lynx Opaque Text under the direction of She Reads Truth and He Reads Truth. The cover is 100# matte with a soft touch aqueous coating.

@SHEREADSTRUTH

@HEREADSTRUTH

SHEREADSTRUTH.COM

HEREADSTRUTH.COM

Download the She Reads Truth and He Reads Truth apps, available for iOS and Android.

All photography used by permission.

ISBN 978-1-949526-49-3

All Scripture is taken from the Christian Standard Bible®. Copyright © 2017 by Holman Bible Publishers. Used by permission. Christian Standard Bible® and CSB® are federally registered trademarks of Holman Bible Publishers.

Research support provided by Logos Bible Software™. Learn more at logos.com.

Though the dates in this book have been carefully researched, scholars disagree on the dating of many biblical events.

THE ACTS OF THE APOSTLES

"But you will receive power when the Holy Spirit has come on you, and you will be my witnesses in Jerusalem, in all Judea and Samaria, and to the end of the earth."

ACTS 1:8

A cts opens with instructions for the early disciples to get up and go "to the end of the earth." The Church was young, and God was teaching them to share the good news of salvation.

For many of us, this "get up and go" command can be frightening or even exhausting to think about. But we forget that the injunction to share the gospel comes with a promise: you will receive power from the Holy Spirit. Jesus sends us out as His witnesses, but we do not go alone.

In this six-week study, we'll read through the entire book of Acts and discover God's plan for His Church. You'll find supplemental readings each day to help you understand Acts in the broader context of Scripture. Each day closes with space for you to reflect on the reading, and each week ends with discussion questions for your group to work through together. Additional resources, like a timeline of the early Church and a look at some of the ways Acts connects to the Gospel of Luke, are included to facilitate deeper engagement with God's Word.

The birth of the early Church is *our* story. This is where we came from, and it points to where we are going. It's the story of how Jesus calls us to reach out and come together. As you read from God's Word, ask the Holy Spirit to guide you, illuminating the words He has already inspired. He is faithful to meet you there, and faithful to give you courage to share. ❧

THE SHE READS TRUTH AND HE READS TRUTH TEAM

DESIGN
ON
PURPOSE

At She Reads Truth and He Reads Truth, we believe in pairing the inherently beautiful Word of God with the aesthetic beauty it deserves. Each of our resources is thoughtfully and artfully designed to highlight the beauty, goodness, and truth of Scripture in a way that reflects the themes of each curated reading plan.

We chose yellow as our main color for this book—a vibrant hue representing the movement and energy of the early Church. The red accents in the color palette call to mind the life-giving blood of Jesus, the foundation on which the Church is built.

The photography is centered around urban life, showing travel, gatherings, and meeting spaces. We selected photos with cool, dark tones to balance the bright, warm colors of the primary color palette.

HOW TO USE THIS BOOK

THE SHE READS TRUTH AND HE READS TRUTH COMMUNITIES ARE DEDICATED TO READING THE WORD OF GOD EVERY DAY.

This Acts reading plan is a journey through all twenty-eight chapters of the book of Acts, with supplemental Scripture passages to help you grasp meaning and biblical context along the way.

SCRIPTURE READING

Designed for a Monday start, this study book presents the book of Acts in daily readings, with supplemental passages for additional context. Each weekday closes with questions for personal reflection and response.

The "you are here" icon in the top corner will help you follow the main events from each reading in Acts on the timeline (p. 116) and on the map (p. 18).

GRACE DAY

Use Saturdays to pray, rest, and reflect on what you've read.

WEEKLY TRUTH

Sundays are set aside for weekly Scripture memorization. The Weekly Truths in this plan are taken from Paul's sermon in Acts 17.

For added community and conversation, join us in the **Acts of the Apostles** reading plan on the She Reads Truth and He Reads Truth apps.

EXTRAS

This book features bonus resources to help you gain a deeper understanding of the text.

THEY ALL JOINED TOGETHER

At the end of each week, you'll find an opportunity for group study. Each group time includes a Scripture selection from the book of Acts and a set of corresponding discussion questions.

GROUP GATHERING GUIDE

The Gathering Guide on page 136 includes six recipes and three hymns you can incorporate into your group time.

TABLE OF CONTENTS

"BUT YOU WILL RECEIVE POWER WHEN THE HOLY SPIRIT HAS COME ON YOU, AND YOU WILL BE MY WITNESSES IN JERUSALEM, IN ALL JUDEA AND SAMARIA, AND TO THE END OF THE EARTH."

KEY VERSE: ACTS 1:8

ON THE TIMELINE

The book of Acts is traditionally credited to a physician named Luke, the author of the Gospel of Luke and a traveling companion of Paul. Luke and Acts are believed to have been written at the same time, during the early to mid AD 60s, likely during Paul's imprisonment in Rome. The events recorded in Acts took place after the death of Christ in AD 33 and conclude in AD 62.

A LITTLE BACKGROUND

Acts provides biographical glimpses of some of the early apostles as they spread the gospel first in Jerusalem and then to the world around the Mediterranean. Peter, Philip, and a few others were responsible for the Church's spread from Jerusalem into Judea and Samaria, while Paul primarily focused on ministry to the Gentiles.

Paul's typical missionary strategy was to go to a familiar place in each city he visited, usually a synagogue, and proclaim the gospel first to local Jews. The speed with which he shifted his focus to Gentiles outside the synagogue depended on how Jews received him within the synagogue. Before leaving a town, Paul united Jewish and Gentile converts to form a local church.

MESSAGE & PURPOSE

The book of Acts emphasizes the work of God through the Holy Spirit in the lives of people who devoted themselves to Jesus Christ, especially Paul as he led the Gentile missionary endeavor. The Christian church was built, city by city, through the dynamic power of the Spirit working through chosen vessels.

GIVE THANKS FOR THE BOOK OF ACTS

The book of Acts ties together the other books of the New Testament by continuing the story begun in the Gospels. Jesus's story did not end with His ascension to heaven forty days after His resurrection; it continued through the lives of His followers. Acts shows us how Jesus's call to take the gospel into the world was carried out by the apostles and other believers by the power of the Holy Spirit. It also gives us the context for much of the New Testament, especially the letters Paul wrote to the churches he helped establish during his missionary journeys.

INTRODUCTION TO THE BOOK OF ACTS

The book of Acts is the story of how the Church began to make its way around the world and through time to the places where we live and worship today.

THE NARRATIVE ARC OF THE BIBLE IS TOLD IN ESSENTIALLY FOUR MOVEMENTS:

EARLY HISTORY

The story of our creation and fall, and God's promise to redeem the world.

THE PEOPLE OF ISRAEL

The story of the nation God set apart in order to bless the world.

THE GOSPELS

The story of God's promises fulfilled through Christ's life, death, and resurrection.

ACTS, LETTERS, AND REVELATION

The story of the first Christians and how the gospel makes all things new.

PEOPLE GROUPS IN ACTS

The gospel of Jesus Christ unifies people separated by culture, race, gender, and social standing. For those living in the Roman Empire of the first century, this unity was unusual and astonishing. Acts repeatedly calls attention to this theme by identifying people not just by name, but by their people group, demonstrating how the gospel unifies.

THERE ARE SIX KEY PEOPLE GROUPS IN THE BOOK OF ACTS:

JEWS / HEBREWS / ISRAELITES

Descendants of Abraham with whom God made a covenant.

Devoted to the law given to Moses at Mount Sinai.

SAMARITANS

Descendants of Israelites from the northern kingdom of Israel who intermarried with Gentiles after the Assyrian Empire repopulated the region.

Had little contact with Jews because of ethnic and religious differences.

GENTILES

Literally, "the nations," or everyone who was not Jewish.

Regarded by most Israelites as unclean.

GOD-FEARERS

Gentiles who worshiped Israel's God but had not fully converted to the Jewish faith.

Did not necessarily adhere to Old Testament laws about food restrictions or circumcision.

ROMANS

Citizens protected by Roman law and granted additional legal rights in the Roman Empire.

Obtained citizenship by birth or legal decree.

GREEKS

People born in Greece, or Greek-speaking people living in the eastern part of the Roman Empire.

PLACES IN ACTS

In the Great Commission, Jesus told His followers they would be His witnesses "in Jerusalem, in all Judea and Samaria, and to the end of the earth" (Ac 1:8). In the first century, many considered the Roman Empire to reach the ends of the earth. In this sense, the progression Jesus described is precisely what happens in the book of Acts as the gospel spreads from Jerusalem, Judea, and Samaria, to the ends of the Roman Empire.

JERUSALEM
Roughly the same city as the one established during King David's reign. As Israel's capital city, Jerusalem was the heart of Jewish history and culture.

JUDEA
South of Samaria, stretching from the Jordan River and Dead Sea west to the Mediterranean Sea.

SAMARIA
Reaching from the Jordan River west to the Mediterranean Sea. Samaria was home to descendants of the Israelites who intermarried with people from other nations after the Assyrians repopulated the region. Samaritans were shunned by many traditional Jewish people.

ASIA MINOR
Modern-day Turkey and Syria. Asia Minor included the regions of Phrygia, Pisidia, Galatia, Cappadocia, and Cilicia, and the cities of Derbe, Lystra, Ephesus, Colossae, Miletus, Philadelphia, and Antioch.

MACEDONIA & ACHAIA
Modern-day Romania, Serbia, Bulgaria, Macedonia, and Greece. The regions of Macedonia and Achaia include the cities of Thessalonica, Philippi, Berea, Athens, and Corinth.

ITALY, SICILY & MALTA
Rome was the capital city of the vast Roman Empire. Sicily and Malta are two islands off the coast of Italy.

ISRAEL UNDER ROMAN RULE

Legend holds that brothers Romulus and Remus founded Rome in 753 BC, and that the first seven kings of Rome increased the size of the kingdom by conquering neighboring territories. The last of these kings, Tarquinius Superbus, was reportedly so tyrannical that the people revolted and established Rome as a republic. As a republic, Rome grew even more powerful, reaching well beyond the borders of Italy into Africa, Asia, and Europe.

When the Roman general Pompey captured Jerusalem in 63 BC, the region of Judea became a territory under Roman rule after almost a century of Jewish independence. Local governance was entrusted in part to local rulers loyal to the Roman Empire, like Herod the Great, and in part to procurators (or governors) appointed by Rome, like Pilate, Felix, and Festus.

The Jewish people were defined by their worship, temple practices, and history as followers of one God, and one God only. Rome granted them an exemption from worshiping Roman gods, allowing Jewish people throughout the empire to practice their monotheistic religion as long as they obeyed Roman rule, paid their taxes, and did not disturb the peace. Jewish people were also excused from military service and from appearing in court on the Sabbath.

Under this arrangement, many in Judea came to see their right to freely worship God as a privilege granted by Rome, one that could be taken away if they fell out of line. This is evident during the Triumphal Entry, when Jewish religious leaders pleaded with Jesus to tell those laying down their palm branches and coats to stop referring to Him as a king. If Roman authorities heard this was happening, they might have shut down the Passover celebration or intervened more extensively in the region (Lk 19:37-40).

Throughout the book of Acts, the land of Israel remained part of Rome. During the New Testament era, the Roman Empire ruled most of the world known to the New Testament audience. 🔖

CHRISTIANITY IN ROME

Christianity was born in the Roman Empire. The book of Acts tells how the message of Christ spread throughout the Roman world not only through missionary journeys, but also by word of mouth from people whose lives had been transformed by the gospel.

The message of Christ spread quickly, and the number of those who believed grew to a size that caught Rome's attention. Early on, the Roman Empire regarded Christianity as a sect of Judaism, which is why Rome tended to treat conflicts between Jews and Christians as internal religious debates (Ac 18:12-17).

Early Christians did not oppose Roman authority. Jesus taught His followers to pay their taxes (Mk 12:17). Paul and the other apostles taught that Christians should honor the government, so long as Roman authorities didn't forbid them from following Christ (1Tm 2:1-2; 1Pt 2:17). Because of this, early Roman persecution of Christians was more the exception than the rule.

There were, however, a few notably tumultuous periods. During the time covered by the book of Acts, Emperor Claudius expelled Jews (and, because Christianity was still regarded as a sect of Judaism, Christians) from Rome. Later, in AD 64, Emperor Nero blamed Christians for the Great Fire of Rome. It may have been during Nero's persecution that both Paul and Peter lost their lives.

Christianity spread throughout the Roman Empire and, according to Romans 15:22-28, a Christian church existed in the city of Rome as early as AD 50—only about twenty years after the death and resurrection of Jesus. The Roman occupation of Judea—something most Israelites viewed as a hardship—set the stage for the gospel to spread from Jerusalem, Judea, and Samaria to the ends of the known earth. 🔖

ASCENSION

Day 1

ACTS 1

PROLOGUE

¹ I wrote the first narrative, Theophilus, about all that Jesus began to do and teach ² until the day he was taken up, after he had given instructions through the Holy Spirit to the apostles he had chosen. ³ After he had suffered, he also presented himself alive to them by many convincing proofs, appearing to them over a period of forty days and speaking about the kingdom of God.

THE HOLY SPIRIT PROMISED

⁴ While he was with them, he commanded them not to leave Jerusalem, but to wait for the Father's promise. "Which," he said, "you have heard me speak about; ⁵ for John baptized with water, but you will be baptized with the Holy Spirit in a few days."

⁶ So when they had come together, they asked him, "Lord, are you restoring the kingdom to Israel at this time?"

⁷ He said to them, "It is not for you to know times or periods that the Father has set by his own authority. ⁸ But you will receive power when the

(+) DID YOU KNOW...

Jesus's last recorded
words before His
ascension are not
found in the four
Gospels, but here
in Acts 1:7-8.

Holy Spirit has come on you, and you will be my witnesses in Jerusalem, in all Judea and Samaria, and to the end of the earth."

THE ASCENSION

⁹ After he had said this, he was taken up as they were watching, and a cloud took him out of their sight. ¹⁰ While he was going, they were gazing into heaven, and suddenly two men in white clothes stood by them. ¹¹ They said, "Men of Galilee, why do you stand looking up into heaven? This same Jesus, who has been taken from you into heaven, will come in the same way that you have seen him going into heaven."

UNITED IN PRAYER

¹² Then they returned to Jerusalem from the Mount of Olives, which is near Jerusalem—a Sabbath day's journey away. ¹³ When they arrived, they went to the room upstairs where they were staying: Peter, John, James, Andrew, Philip, Thomas, Bartholomew, Matthew, James the son of Alphaeus, Simon the Zealot, and Judas the son of James. ¹⁴ They all were continually united in prayer, along with the women, including Mary the mother of Jesus, and his brothers.

MATTHIAS CHOSEN

¹⁵ In those days Peter stood up among the brothers and sisters—the number of people who were together was about a hundred and twenty— and said: ¹⁶ "Brothers and sisters, it was necessary that the Scripture be fulfilled that the Holy Spirit through the mouth of David foretold about Judas, who became a guide to those who arrested Jesus. ¹⁷ For he was one of our number and shared in this ministry." ¹⁸ Now this man acquired a field with his unrighteous wages. He fell headfirst, his body burst open and his intestines spilled out. ¹⁹ This became known to all the residents of Jerusalem, so that in their own language that field is called Hakeldama (that is, Field of Blood). ²⁰ "For it is written in the Book of Psalms:

Let his dwelling become desolate;
let no one live in it; and
Let someone else take his position.

²¹ "Therefore, from among the men who have accompanied us during the whole time the Lord Jesus went in and out among us— ²² beginning from the baptism of John until the day he was taken up from us—from among these, it is necessary that one become a witness with us of his resurrection."

²³ So they proposed two: Joseph, called Barsabbas, who was also known as Justus, and Matthias. ²⁴ Then they prayed, "You, Lord, know everyone's hearts; show which of these two you have chosen ²⁵ to take the place in this apostolic ministry that Judas left to go where he belongs." ²⁶ Then they cast lots for them, and the lot fell to Matthias and he was added to the eleven apostles.

MATTHEW 28:16-20

THE GREAT COMMISSION

¹⁶ The eleven disciples traveled to Galilee, to the mountain where Jesus had directed them. ¹⁷ When they saw him, they worshiped, but some doubted. ¹⁸ Jesus came near and said to them, "All authority has been given to me in heaven and on earth. ¹⁹ Go, therefore, and make disciples of all nations, baptizing them in the name of the Father and of the Son and of the Holy Spirit, ²⁰ teaching them to observe everything I have commanded you. And remember, I am with you always, to the end of the age."

ROMANS 6:11-14

¹¹ So, you too consider yourselves dead to sin and alive to God in Christ Jesus.

¹² Therefore do not let sin reign in your mortal body, so that you obey its desires. ¹³ And do not offer any parts of it to sin as weapons for unrighteousness. But as those who are alive from the dead, offer yourselves to God, and all the parts of yourselves to God as weapons for righteousness. ¹⁴ For sin will not rule over you, because you are not under the law but under grace.

RESPONSE

Day 1

What did you notice
about this passage?

What does this teach
you about God?

How does this lead
you to pray?

How are you
challenged to
live differently?

THE COMING OF THE HOLY SPIRIT

Day 2

ACTS 2

PENTECOST

¹ When the day of Pentecost had arrived, they were all together in one place. ² Suddenly a sound like that of a violent rushing wind came from heaven, and it filled the whole house where they were staying. ³ They saw tongues like flames of fire that separated and rested on each one of them. ⁴ Then they were all filled with the Holy Spirit and began to speak in different tongues, as the Spirit enabled them.

⁵ Now there were Jews staying in Jerusalem, devout people from every nation under heaven. ⁶ When this sound occurred, a crowd came together and was confused because each one heard them speaking in his own language. ⁷ They were astounded and amazed, saying, "Look, aren't all these who are speaking Galileans? ⁸ How is it that each of us can hear them in our own native language? ⁹ Parthians, Medes, Elamites; those who live in Mesopotamia, in Judea and Cappadocia, Pontus and Asia, ¹⁰ Phrygia and Pamphylia, Egypt and the parts of Libya near Cyrene; visitors from Rome (both Jews and converts), ¹¹ Cretans and Arabs—we hear them declaring the magnificent acts of God in our own tongues." ¹² They were

all astounded and perplexed, saying to one another, "What does this mean?" ¹³ But some sneered and said, "They're drunk on new wine."

PETER'S SERMON

¹⁴ Peter stood up with the Eleven, raised his voice, and proclaimed to them: "Fellow Jews and all you residents of Jerusalem, let me explain this to you and pay attention to my words. ¹⁵ For these people are not drunk, as you suppose, since it's only nine in the morning. ¹⁶ On the contrary, this is what was spoken through the prophet Joel:

> ¹⁷ And it will be in the last days, says God,
> that I will pour out my Spirit on all people;
> then your sons and your daughters will prophesy,
> your young men will see visions,
> and your old men will dream dreams.
> ¹⁸ I will even pour out my Spirit
> on my servants in those days, both men and women
> and they will prophesy.
> ¹⁹ I will display wonders in the heaven above
> and signs on the earth below:
> blood and fire and a cloud of smoke.
> ²⁰ The sun will be turned to darkness
> and the moon to blood
> before the great and glorious day of the Lord comes.
> ²¹ Then everyone who calls
> on the name of the Lord will be saved.

²² "Fellow Israelites, listen to these words: This Jesus of Nazareth was a man attested to you by God with miracles, wonders, and signs that God did among you through him, just as you yourselves know. ²³ Though he was delivered up according to God's determined plan and foreknowledge, you used lawless people to nail him to a cross and kill him. ²⁴ God raised him up, ending the pains of death, because it was not possible for him to be held by death. ²⁵ For David says of him:

> I saw the Lord ever before me;
> because he is at my right hand,
> I will not be shaken.
> ²⁶ Therefore my heart is glad
> and my tongue rejoices.

Moreover, my flesh will rest in hope,

27 because you will not abandon me
   in Hades
or allow your holy one to see decay.

28 You have revealed the paths of life to me;
you will fill me with gladness
   in your presence.

29 "Brothers and sisters, I can confidently speak to you about the patriarch David: He is both dead and buried, and his tomb is with us to this day. 30 Since he was a prophet, he knew that God had sworn an oath to him to seat one of his descendants on his throne. 31 Seeing what was to come, he spoke concerning the resurrection of the Messiah: He was not abandoned in Hades, and his flesh did not experience decay.

32 "God has raised this Jesus; we are all witnesses of this. 33 Therefore, since he has been exalted to the right hand of God and has received from the Father the promised Holy Spirit, he has poured out what you both see and hear. 34 For it was not David who ascended into the heavens, but he himself says:

The Lord declared to my Lord,
'Sit at my right hand
35 until I make your enemies your footstool.'

36 "Therefore let all the house of Israel know with certainty that God has made this Jesus, whom you crucified, both Lord and Messiah."

CALL TO REPENTANCE

37 When they heard this, they were pierced to the heart and said to Peter and the rest of the apostles: "Brothers, what should we do?"

38 Peter replied, "Repent and be baptized, each of you, in the name of Jesus Christ for the forgiveness of your sins, and you will receive the gift of the Holy Spirit. 39 For the promise is for you and for your children, and for all who are far off, as many as the Lord our God will call." 40 With many other words he testified and strongly urged them, saying, "Be saved from this corrupt generation!" 41 So those who accepted his message were baptized, and that day about three thousand people were added to them.

A GENEROUS AND GROWING CHURCH

42 They devoted themselves to the apostles' teaching, to the fellowship, to the breaking of bread, and to prayer.

43 Everyone was filled with awe, and many wonders and signs were being performed through the apostles. 44 Now all the believers were together and held all things in common. 45 They sold their possessions and property and distributed the proceeds to all, as any had need. 46 Every day they devoted themselves to meeting together in the temple, and broke bread from house to house. They ate their food with joyful and sincere hearts, 47 praising God and enjoying the favor of all the people. Every day the Lord added to their number those who were being saved.

JOEL 2:28-32

GOD'S PROMISE OF HIS SPIRIT

28 "After this
I will pour out my Spirit on all humanity;
then your sons and your daughters
   will prophesy,
your old men will have dreams,
and your young men will see visions.

²⁹ I will even pour out my Spirit
on the male and female slaves in those days.
³⁰ I will display wonders
in the heavens and on the earth:
blood, fire, and columns of smoke.
³¹ The sun will be turned to darkness
and the moon to blood
before the great and terrible day of the LORD comes.

³² Then everyone who calls
on the name of the LORD will be saved,

for there will be an escape
for those on Mount Zion and in Jerusalem,
as the LORD promised,
among the survivors the LORD calls."

PSALM 16:8-11

⁸ I always let the LORD guide me.
Because he is at my right hand,
I will not be shaken.

⁹ Therefore my heart is glad
and my whole being rejoices;
my body also rests securely.
¹⁰ For you will not abandon me to Sheol;
you will not allow your faithful one to see decay.
¹¹ You reveal the path of life to me;
in your presence is abundant joy;
at your right hand are eternal pleasures.

RESPONSE

Day 2

What did you notice
about this passage?

What does this teach
you about God?

How does this lead
you to pray?

How are you
challenged to
live differently?

KEY

SEQUENCE LISTED IN ACTS 2:9–11

APPROXIMATE LOCATION OF MAJOR NATIONS LISTED IN GENESIS 10

GOMER

13
ROME

TIRAS

Adriatic Sea

JAVAN

8
ASIA

Mediterranean Sea

CAPHTOR

14
CRETE

CYRENE

PUT

12
CYRENE

THE PLACES OF PENTECOST

At Pentecost, the Holy Spirit fell upon the disciples gathered in the upper room and gave them supernatural ability to speak in foreign languages. Jewish men and women "from every nation under heaven" who had come to Jerusalem for the festival heard their own tongues spoken and were amazed. They accepted the truth about Jesus and brought the gospel back home with them.

The list of places named in Acts 2 is more than just a roster of attendance; it loosely reflects the nations in Genesis 10—nations that represented the entirety of the known world. With the birth of the Church, a people defined by loyalty to Jesus Christ and the presence of the Holy Spirit rather than geography, God began the work of reclaiming the dispersed nations of the world as His own possession.

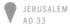

CHRIST GIVES PETER POWER TO HEAL

Day 3

ACTS 3

HEALING OF A LAME MAN

¹ Now Peter and John were going up to the temple for the time of prayer at three in the afternoon. ² A man who was lame from birth was being carried there. He was placed each day at the temple gate called Beautiful, so that he could beg from those entering the temple. ³ When he saw Peter and John about to enter the temple, he asked for money. ⁴ Peter, along with John, looked straight at him and said, "Look at us." ⁵ So he turned to them, expecting to get something from them. ⁶ But Peter said,

"I don't have silver or gold, but what I do have, I give you: In the name of Jesus Christ of Nazareth, get up and walk!"

⁷ Then, taking him by the right hand he raised him up, and at once his feet and ankles became strong. ⁸ So he jumped up and started to walk, and he entered the temple with them—walking, leaping, and praising God. ⁹ All the people saw him walking and praising God, ¹⁰ and they recognized that he was the one who used to sit and beg at the Beautiful

Gate of the temple. So they were filled with awe and astonishment at what had happened to him.

PREACHING IN SOLOMON'S COLONNADE

[11] While he was holding on to Peter and John, all the people, utterly astonished, ran toward them in what is called Solomon's Colonnade. [12] When Peter saw this, he addressed the people: "Fellow Israelites, why are you amazed at this? Why do you stare at us, as though we had made him walk by our own power or godliness? [13] The God of Abraham, Isaac, and Jacob, the God of our ancestors, has glorified his servant Jesus, whom you handed over and denied before Pilate, though he had decided to release him. [14] You denied the Holy and Righteous One and asked to have a murderer released to you. [15] You killed the source of life, whom God raised from the dead; we are witnesses of this. [16] By faith in his name, his name has made this man strong, whom you see and know. So the faith that comes through Jesus has given him this perfect health in front of all of you.

[17] "And now, brothers and sisters, I know that you acted in ignorance, just as your leaders also did. [18] In this way God fulfilled what he had predicted through all the prophets—that his Messiah would suffer. [19] Therefore repent and turn back, so that your sins may be wiped out, [20] that seasons of refreshing may come from the presence of the Lord, and that he may send Jesus, who has been appointed for you as the Messiah. [21] Heaven must receive him until the time of the restoration of all things, which God spoke about through his holy prophets from the beginning. [22] Moses said: The Lord your God will raise up for you a prophet like me from among your brothers and sisters. You must listen to everything he tells you. [23] And everyone who does not listen to that prophet will be completely cut off from the people.

[24] "In addition, all the prophets who have spoken, from Samuel and those after him, have also foretold these days. [25] You are the sons of the prophets and of the covenant that God made with your ancestors, saying to Abraham, And all the families of the earth will be blessed through your offspring. [26] God raised up his servant and sent him first to you to bless you by turning each of you from your evil ways."

RESURRECTION ESSENTIAL TO THE GOSPEL

¹ Now I want to make clear for you, brothers and sisters, the gospel I preached to you, which you received, on which you have taken your stand ² and by which you are being saved, if you hold to the message I preached to you—unless you believed in vain. ³ For I passed on to you as most important what I also received: that Christ died for our sins according to the Scriptures, ⁴ that he was buried, that he was raised on the third day according to the Scriptures…

DEUTERONOMY 18:15–19

¹⁵ The Lord your God will raise up for you a prophet like me from among your own brothers. You must listen to him. ¹⁶ This is what you requested from the Lord your God at Horeb on the day of the assembly when you said, "Let us not continue to hear the voice of the Lord our God or see this great fire any longer, so that we will not die!" ¹⁷ Then the Lord said to me, "They have spoken well. ¹⁸ I will raise up for them a prophet like you from among their brothers. I will put my words in his mouth, and he will tell them everything I command him. ¹⁹ I will hold accountable whoever does not listen to my words that he speaks in my name."

RESPONSE

Day 3

What did you notice
about this passage?

What does this teach
you about God?

How does this lead
you to pray?

4

How are you
challenged to
live differently?

NO OTHER NAME

Day 4

ACTS 4:1–22

PETER AND JOHN ARRESTED

[1] While they were speaking to the people, the priests, the captain of the temple police, and the Sadducees confronted them, [2] because they were annoyed that they were teaching the people and proclaiming in Jesus the resurrection of the dead. [3] So they seized them and took them into custody until the next day since it was already evening. [4] But many of those who heard the message believed, and the number of the men came to about five thousand.

PETER AND JOHN FACE THE JEWISH LEADERSHIP

[5] The next day, their rulers, elders, and scribes assembled in Jerusalem [6] with Annas the high priest, Caiaphas, John, Alexander, and all the members of the high-priestly family. [7] After they had Peter and John stand before them, they began to question them:

"By what power or in what name have you done this?"

[8] Then Peter was filled with the Holy Spirit and said to them, "Rulers of the people and elders: [9] If we are being examined today about a good deed done to a disabled man, by what means he was healed, [10] let it be known to all of you and to all the people of Israel, that by the name of Jesus Christ of Nazareth, whom you crucified and whom God raised from the dead—by him this man is standing here before you healthy. [11] This Jesus is

> the stone rejected by you builders,
> which has become the cornerstone.

[12] There is salvation in no one else, for there is no other name under heaven given to people by which we must be saved."

THE BOLDNESS OF THE DISCIPLES

[13] When they observed the boldness of Peter and John and realized that they were uneducated and untrained men, they were amazed and recognized that they had been with Jesus. [14] And since they saw the man who had been healed standing with them, they had nothing to say in opposition. [15] After they ordered them to leave the Sanhedrin, they conferred among themselves, [16] saying, "What should we do with these men? For an obvious sign has been done through them, clear to everyone living in Jerusalem, and we cannot deny it. [17] But so that this does not spread any further among the people, let's threaten them against speaking to anyone in this name again." [18] So they called for them and ordered them not to speak or teach at all in the name of Jesus.

[19] Peter and John answered them, "Whether it's right in the sight of God for us to listen to you rather than to God, you decide; [20] for we are unable to stop speaking about what we have seen and heard."

[21] After threatening them further, they released them. They found no way to punish them because the people were all giving glory to God over what had been done. [22] For this sign of healing had been performed on a man over forty years old.

2 CORINTHIANS 3:12–18

[12] Since, then, we have such a hope, we act with great boldness. [13] We are not like Moses, who used to put a veil over his face to prevent the Israelites from gazing steadily until the end of the glory of what was being

set aside, [14] but their minds were hardened. For to this day, at the reading of the old covenant, the same veil remains; it is not lifted, because it is set aside only in Christ. [15] Yet still today, whenever Moses is read, a veil lies over their hearts, [16] but whenever a person turns to the Lord, the veil is removed. [17] Now the Lord is the Spirit, and where the Spirit of the Lord is, there is freedom. [18] We all, with unveiled faces, are looking as in a mirror at the glory of the Lord and are being transformed into the same image from glory to glory; this is from the Lord who is the Spirit.

1 JOHN 5:12

The one who has the Son has life. The one who does not have the Son of God does not have life.

RESPONSE

Day 4

What did you notice
about this passage?

What does this teach
you about God?

How does this lead
you to pray?

How are you
challenged to
live differently?

THE EFFECTS OF THE GOSPEL

Day 5

ACTS 4:23–37

PRAYER FOR BOLDNESS

²³ After they were released, they went to their own people and reported everything the chief priests and the elders had said to them. ²⁴ When they heard this, they raised their voices together to God and said, "Master, you are the one who made the heaven, the earth, and the sea, and everything in them. ²⁵ You said through the Holy Spirit, by the mouth of our father David your servant:

> Why do the Gentiles rage
> and the peoples plot futile things?
> ²⁶ The kings of the earth take their stand
> and the rulers assemble together
> against the Lord and against his Messiah.

²⁷ "For, in fact, in this city both Herod and Pontius Pilate, with the Gentiles and the people of Israel, assembled together against your holy servant Jesus, whom you anointed, ²⁸ to do whatever your hand and your will had predestined to take place. ²⁹ And now, Lord, consider their threats, and grant that your servants may speak your word with all

boldness, [30] while you stretch out your hand for healing, and signs and wonders are performed through the name of your holy servant Jesus."

[31] When they had prayed, the place where they were assembled was shaken, and they were all filled with the Holy Spirit and began to speak the word of God boldly.

ALL THINGS IN COMMON

[32] Now the entire group of those who believed were of one heart and mind, and no one claimed that any of his possessions was his own, but instead they held everything in common. [33] With great power the apostles were giving testimony to the resurrection of the Lord Jesus, and great grace was on all of them. [34] For there was not a needy person among them because all those who owned lands or houses sold them, brought the proceeds of what was sold, [35] and laid them at the apostles' feet. This was then distributed to each person as any had need.

[36] Joseph, a Levite from Cyprus by birth, the one the apostles called Barnabas (which is translated Son of Encouragement), [37] sold a field he owned, brought the money, and laid it at the apostles' feet.

ACTS 5:1–16

LYING TO THE HOLY SPIRIT

[1] But a man named Ananias, with his wife Sapphira, sold a piece of property. [2] However, he kept back part of the proceeds with his wife's knowledge, and brought a portion of it and laid it at the apostles' feet.

[3] "Ananias," Peter asked, "why has Satan filled your heart to lie to the Holy Spirit and keep back part of the proceeds of the land? [4] Wasn't it yours while you possessed it? And after it was sold, wasn't it at your disposal? Why is it that you planned this thing in your heart? You have not lied to people but to God." [5] When he heard these words, Ananias dropped dead, and a great fear came on all who heard. [6] The young men got up, wrapped his body, carried him out, and buried him.

[7] About three hours later, his wife came in, not knowing what had happened. [8] "Tell me," Peter asked her, "did you sell the land for this price?"

NOTES

SHE READS TRUTH | HE READS TRUTH   49

"Yes," she said, "for that price."

⁹ Then Peter said to her, "Why did you agree to test the Spirit of the Lord? Look, the feet of those who have buried your husband are at the door, and they will carry you out."

¹⁰ Instantly she dropped dead at his feet. When the young men came in, they found her dead, carried her out, and buried her beside her husband. ¹¹ Then great fear came on the whole church and on all who heard these things.

APOSTOLIC SIGNS AND WONDERS

¹² Many signs and wonders were being done among the people through the hands of the apostles. They were all together in Solomon's Colonnade. ¹³ No one else dared to join them, but the people spoke well of them. ¹⁴ Believers were added to the Lord in increasing numbers—multitudes of both men and women. ¹⁵ As a result, they would carry the sick out into the streets and lay them on cots and mats so that when Peter came by, at least his shadow might fall on some of them. ¹⁶ In addition, a multitude came together from the towns surrounding Jerusalem, bringing the sick and those who were tormented by unclean spirits, and they were all healed.

DEUTERONOMY 15:4–6

⁴ "There will be no poor among you, however, because the Lord is certain to bless you in the land the Lord your God is giving you to possess as an inheritance— ⁵ if only you obey the Lord your God and are careful to follow every one of these commands I am giving you today. ⁶ When the Lord your God blesses you as he has promised you, you will lend to many nations but not borrow; you will rule many nations, but they will not rule you."

HEBREWS 6:13–20

INHERITING THE PROMISE

¹³ For when God made a promise to Abraham, since he had no one greater to swear by, he swore by himself: ¹⁴ I will indeed bless you, and I will greatly multiply you. ¹⁵ And so, after waiting patiently, Abraham obtained the promise. ¹⁶ For people swear by something greater than

themselves, and for them a confirming oath ends every dispute. [17] Because God wanted to show his unchangeable purpose even more clearly to the heirs of the promise, he guaranteed it with an oath, [18] so that through two unchangeable things, in which it is impossible for God to lie, we who have fled for refuge might have strong encouragement to seize the hope set before us. [19] We have this hope as an anchor for the soul, firm and secure. It enters the inner sanctuary behind the curtain. [20] Jesus has entered there on our behalf as a forerunner, because he has become a high priest forever according to the order of Melchizedek.

RESPONSE

Day 5

What did you notice
about this passage?

What does this teach
you about God?

How does this lead
you to pray?

How are you
challenged to
live differently?

Week 1

THEY ALL JOINED TOGETHER

In the spirit of Acts 2:42, choose a time to gather with a group to read Scripture aloud and discuss the text together. Like the earliest believers who faithfully gathered together in the name of Christ and His gospel, we can make space to pray and read Scripture with one another.

TURN TO PAGE 29 AND READ ACTS 2:14–36 OUT LOUD TOGETHER. DISCUSS THE PASSAGE USING THE QUESTIONS PROVIDED.

CHECK OUT THE GATHERING GUIDE ON PAGE 136 FOR RECIPE AND HYMN IDEAS TO INCORPORATE INTO YOUR GROUP TIME!

QUESTIONS

1. What do you notice about this passage?

2. Peter declared the wonderful works of God, even though he denied Christ before the crucifixion (Lk 22:54-62). What does this teach us about the nature of the gospel?

3. What are the wonderful works of God? What do God's works reveal about His character?

4. Why do you think Peter and the disciples quoted so much Old Testament Scripture?

5. What does Peter's sermon reveal about Christ?

PRAYER

Close your time together by praying for one another.

GRACE DAY

GRACE DAY

GRACE DAY

GRACE DAY

GRACE DAY

GRACE DAY

The early Church was dedicated to prayer. May the same be true of us.

Take this day as an opportunity to catch up on your reading, pray, and rest in the presence of the Lord. Pray Acts 1:14 for yourself and your community.

They all were continually united in prayer, along with the women, including Mary the mother of Jesus, and his brothers.

ACTS 1:14

T R

U

T H

Weekly Truth

Scripture is God-breathed and true. When we memorize it, we carry the gospel with us wherever we go.

As we read through Acts, we will be memorizing Acts 17:24–29, a passage from Paul's eloquent yet succinct presentation of the gospel to the Greek philosophers at the Areopagus. By memorizing one verse per week, we will have all six verses committed to memory by the end of the study. This week's verse is highlighted here.

²⁴ The God who made the world and everything in it—he is Lord of heaven and earth—does not live in shrines made by hands. ²⁵ Neither is he served by human hands, as though he needed anything, since he himself gives everyone life and breath and all things. ²⁶ From one man he has made every nationality to live over the whole earth and has determined their appointed times and the boundaries of where they live. ²⁷ He did this so that they might seek God, and perhaps they might reach out and find him, though he is not far from each one of us. ²⁸ For in him we live and move and have our being, as even some of your own poets have said, "For we are also his offspring." ²⁹ Since we are God's offspring then, we shouldn't think that the divine nature is like gold or silver or stone, an image fashioned by human art and imagination.

THE APOSTLES PREACH THE GOSPEL

Day 8

ACTS 5:17–42

IN AND OUT OF PRISON

¹⁷ Then the high priest rose up. He and all who were with him, who belonged to the party of the Sadducees, were filled with jealousy. ¹⁸ So they arrested the apostles and put them in the public jail. ¹⁹ But an angel of the Lord opened the doors of the jail during the night, brought them out, and said, ²⁰ "Go and stand in the temple, and tell the people all about this life." ²¹ Hearing this, they entered the temple at daybreak and began to teach.

THE APOSTLES ON TRIAL AGAIN

When the high priest and those who were with him arrived, they convened the Sanhedrin—the full council of the Israelites—and sent orders to the jail to have them brought. ²² But when the servants got there, they did not find them in the jail, so they returned and reported, ²³ "We found the jail securely locked, with the guards standing in front of the doors, but when we opened them, we found no one inside." ²⁴ As the captain of the temple police and the chief priests heard these things, they were baffled about them, wondering what would come of this.

²⁵ Someone came and reported to them, "Look! The men you put in jail are standing in the temple and teaching the people." ²⁶ Then the commander went with the servants and brought them in without force, because they were afraid the people might stone them. ²⁷ After they brought them in, they had them stand before the Sanhedrin, and the high priest asked, ²⁸ "Didn't we strictly order you not to teach in this name? Look, you have filled Jerusalem with your teaching and are determined to make us guilty of this man's blood."

²⁹ Peter and the apostles replied,

"We must obey God rather than people.

³⁰ The God of our ancestors raised up Jesus, whom you had murdered by hanging him on a tree. ³¹ God exalted this man to his right hand as ruler and Savior, to give repentance to Israel and forgiveness of sins. ³² We are witnesses of these things, and so is the Holy Spirit whom God has given to those who obey him."

 DID YOU KNOW...

Gamaliel, the respected Pharisee who advised the Sanhedrin to exercise patience, trained a young, zealous Pharisee named Saul, who would later become the apostle Paul (Acts 22:3).

GAMALIEL'S ADVICE

³³ When they heard this, they were enraged and wanted to kill them. ³⁴ But a Pharisee named Gamaliel, a teacher of the law who was respected by all the people, stood up in the Sanhedrin and ordered the men to be taken outside for a little while. ³⁵ He said to them, "Men of Israel, be careful about what you're about to do to these men. ³⁶ Some time ago Theudas rose up, claiming to be somebody, and a group of about four hundred men rallied to him. He was killed, and all his followers were dispersed and came to nothing. ³⁷ After this man, Judas the Galilean rose up in the days of the census and attracted a following. He also perished, and all his followers were scattered. ³⁸ So in the present case, I tell you, stay away from these men and leave them alone. For if this plan or this work is of human origin, it will fail; ³⁹ but if it is of God, you will not be able to overthrow them. You may even be found fighting against God." They were persuaded by him. ⁴⁰ After they called in the apostles and had them flogged, they ordered them not to speak in the name of Jesus and released them. ⁴¹ Then they went out from the presence of the Sanhedrin, rejoicing that they were counted worthy to be treated shamefully on behalf of the Name. ⁴² Every day in the temple, and in various homes, they continued teaching and proclaiming the good news that Jesus is the Messiah.

[6] A voice was saying, "Cry out!"
Another said, "What should I cry out?"
"All humanity is grass,
and all its goodness is like the flower of the field.
[7] The grass withers, the flowers fade
when the breath of the LORD blows on them;
indeed, the people are grass.
[8] The grass withers, the flowers fade,
but the word of our God remains forever."

1 JOHN 2:15-17

A WARNING ABOUT THE WORLD

[15] Do not love the world or the things in the world. If anyone loves the world, the love of the Father is not in him. [16] For everything in the world—the lust of the flesh, the lust of the eyes, and the pride in one's possessions—is not from the Father, but is from the world. [17] And the world with its lust is passing away, but the one who does the will of God remains forever.

RESPONSE

Day 8

What did you notice
about this passage?

What does this teach
you about God?

How does this lead
you to pray?

How are you
challenged to
live differently?

EVIDENCE OF THE SPIRIT'S WORK

Day 9

ACTS 6

SEVEN CHOSEN TO SERVE

¹ In those days, as the disciples were increasing in number, there arose a complaint by the Hellenistic Jews against the Hebraic Jews that their widows were being overlooked in the daily distribution. ² The Twelve summoned the whole company of the disciples and said, "It would not be right for us to give up preaching the word of God to wait on tables. ³ Brothers and sisters, select from among you seven men of good reputation, full of the Spirit and wisdom, whom we can appoint to this duty. ⁴ But we will devote ourselves to prayer and to the ministry of the word." ⁵ This proposal pleased the whole company. So they chose Stephen, a man full of faith and the Holy Spirit, and Philip, Prochorus, Nicanor, Timon, Parmenas, and Nicolaus, a convert from Antioch. ⁶ They had them stand before the apostles, who prayed and laid their hands on them.

⁷ So the word of God spread, the disciples in Jerusalem increased greatly in number, and a large group of priests became obedient to the faith.

STEPHEN ACCUSED OF BLASPHEMY

⁸ Now Stephen, full of grace and power, was performing great wonders and signs among the people. ⁹ Opposition arose, however, from some members of the Freedmen's Synagogue, composed of both Cyrenians and Alexandrians, and some from Cilicia and Asia, and they began to argue with Stephen. ¹⁰ But they were unable to stand up against his wisdom and the Spirit by whom he was speaking.

¹¹ Then they secretly persuaded some men to say, "We heard him speaking blasphemous words against Moses and God." ¹² They stirred up the people, the elders, and the scribes; so they came, seized him, and took him to the Sanhedrin. ¹³ They also presented false witnesses who said, "This man never stops speaking against this holy place and the law. ¹⁴ For we heard him say that this Jesus of Nazareth will destroy this place and change the customs that Moses handed down to us." ¹⁵ And all who were sitting in the Sanhedrin looked intently at him and saw that his face was like the face of an angel.

GENESIS 4:3-7

³ In the course of time Cain presented some of the land's produce as an offering to the LORD. ⁴ And Abel also presented an offering—some of the firstborn of his flock and their fat portions. The LORD had regard for Abel and his offering, ⁵ but he did not have regard for Cain and his offering. Cain was furious, and he looked despondent.

⁶ Then the LORD said to Cain, "Why are you furious? And why do you look despondent? ⁷ If you do what is right, won't you be accepted? But if you do not do what is right, sin is crouching at the door. Its desire is for you, but you must rule over it."

1 TIMOTHY 3:8-13

⁸ Deacons, likewise, should be worthy of respect, not hypocritical, not drinking a lot of wine, not greedy for money, ⁹ holding the mystery of the faith with a clear conscience. ¹⁰ They must also be tested first; if they prove blameless, then they can serve as deacons. ¹¹ Wives, too, must be worthy of respect, not slanderers, self-controlled, faithful in everything. ¹² Deacons are to be husbands of one wife, managing their children and

their own households competently. ¹³ For those who have served well as deacons acquire a good standing for themselves and great boldness in the faith that is in Christ Jesus.

EXODUS 34:29-30

MOSES'S RADIANT FACE

²⁹ As Moses descended from Mount Sinai—with the two tablets of the testimony in his hands as he descended the mountain—he did not realize that the skin of his face shone as a result of his speaking with the LORD. ³⁰ When Aaron and all the Israelites saw Moses, the skin of his face shone! They were afraid to come near him.

RESPONSE

Day 9

1

What did you notice
about this passage?

2

What does this teach
you about God?

3

How does this lead
you to pray?

4

How are you
challenged to
live differently?

STEPHEN'S SERMON

Day 10

ACTS 7:1-53

STEPHEN'S SERMON

[1] "Are these things true?" the high priest asked.

[2] "Brothers and fathers," he replied, "listen: The God of glory appeared to our father Abraham when he was in Mesopotamia, before he settled in Haran, [3] and said to him: Leave your country and relatives, and come to the land that I will show you.

[4] "Then he left the land of the Chaldeans and settled in Haran. From there, after his father died, God had him move to this land in which you are now living. [5] He didn't give him an inheritance in it—not even a foot of ground—but he promised to give it to him as a possession, and to his descendants after him, even though he was childless. [6] God spoke in this way: His descendants would be strangers in a foreign country, and they would enslave and oppress them for four hundred years. [7] I will judge the nation that they will serve as slaves, God said. After this, they will come out and worship me in this place. [8] And so he gave Abraham the covenant of circumcision. After this, he fathered Isaac and circumcised him on the eighth day. Isaac became the father of Jacob, and Jacob became the father of the twelve patriarchs.

[9] "The patriarchs became jealous of Joseph and sold him into Egypt, but God was with him [10] and rescued him out of all his troubles. He gave him favor and wisdom in the sight of Pharaoh, king of Egypt, who appointed him ruler over Egypt and over his whole household. [11] Now a famine and great suffering came over all of Egypt and Canaan, and our ancestors could find no food. [12] When Jacob heard there was grain in Egypt, he sent our ancestors there the first time. [13] The second time, Joseph revealed himself to his brothers, and Joseph's family became known to Pharaoh. [14] Joseph invited his father Jacob and all his relatives, seventy-five people in all, [15] and Jacob went down to Egypt. He and our ancestors died there, [16] were carried back to Shechem, and were placed in the tomb that Abraham had bought for a sum of silver from the sons of Hamor in Shechem.

MOSES, A REJECTED SAVIOR

[17] "As the time was approaching to fulfill the promise that God had made to Abraham, the people flourished and multiplied in Egypt [18] until a different king who did not know Joseph ruled over Egypt. [19] He dealt deceitfully with our race and oppressed our ancestors by making them abandon their infants outside so that they wouldn't survive. [20] At this time Moses was born, and he was beautiful in God's sight. He was cared for in his father's home for three months. [21] When he was put outside, Pharaoh's daughter adopted and raised him as her own son. [22] So Moses was educated in all the wisdom of the Egyptians and was powerful in his speech and actions.

[23] "When he was forty years old, he decided to visit his own people, the Israelites. [24] When he saw one of them being mistreated, he came to his rescue and avenged the oppressed man by striking down the Egyptian. [25] He assumed his people would understand that God would give them deliverance through him, but they did not understand. [26] The next day he showed up while they were fighting and tried to reconcile them peacefully, saying, 'Men, you are brothers. Why are you mistreating each other?'

[27] "But the one who was mistreating his neighbor pushed Moses aside, saying: Who appointed you a ruler and a judge over us? [28] Do you want to kill me, the same way you killed the Egyptian yesterday?

29 "When he heard this, Moses fled and became an exile in the land of Midian, where he became the father of two sons. 30 After forty years had passed, an angel appeared to him in the wilderness of Mount Sinai, in the flame of a burning bush. 31 When Moses saw it, he was amazed at the sight. As he was approaching to look at it, the voice of the Lord came: 32 I am the God of your ancestors—the God of Abraham, of Isaac, and of Jacob. Moses began to tremble and did not dare to look.

33 "The Lord said to him: Take off the sandals from your feet, because the place where you are standing is holy ground. 34 I have certainly seen the oppression of my people in Egypt; I have heard their groaning and have come down to set them free. And now, come, I will send you to Egypt.

35 "This Moses, whom they rejected when they said, Who appointed you a ruler and a judge?—this one God sent as a ruler and a deliverer through the angel who appeared to him in the bush. 36 This man led them out and performed wonders and signs in the land of Egypt, at the Red Sea, and in the wilderness for forty years.

ISRAEL'S REBELLION AGAINST GOD

37 "This is the Moses who said to the Israelites: God will raise up for you a prophet like me from among your brothers and sisters. 38 He is the one who was in the assembly in the wilderness, with the angel who spoke to him on Mount Sinai, and with our ancestors. He received living oracles to give to us. 39 Our ancestors were unwilling to obey him. Instead, they pushed him aside, and in their hearts turned back to Egypt. 40 They told Aaron: Make us gods who will go before us. As for this Moses who brought us out of the land of Egypt, we don't know what's happened to him. 41 They even made a calf in those days, offered sacrifice to the idol, and were celebrating what their hands had made. 42 God turned away and gave them up to worship the stars of heaven, as it is written in the book of the prophets:

> House of Israel, did you bring me offerings and sacrifices
> for forty years in the wilderness?
> 43 You took up the tent of Moloch
> and the star of your god Rephan,
> the images that you made to worship.
> So I will send you into exile beyond Babylon.

[44] "Our ancestors had the tabernacle of the testimony in the wilderness, just as he who spoke to Moses commanded him to make it according to the pattern he had seen. [45] Our ancestors in turn received it and with Joshua brought it in when they dispossessed the nations that God drove out before them, until the days of David. [46] He found favor in God's sight and asked that he might provide a dwelling place for the God of Jacob. [47] It was Solomon, rather, who built him a house, [48] but the Most High does not dwell in sanctuaries made with hands, as the prophet says:

[49] Heaven is my throne,
and the earth my footstool.
What sort of house will you build for me?
says the Lord,
or what will be my resting place?
[50] Did not my hand make all these things?

RESISTING THE HOLY SPIRIT

[51] "You stiff-necked people with uncircumcised hearts and ears! You are always resisting the Holy Spirit. As your ancestors did, you do also. [52] Which of the prophets did your ancestors not persecute? They even killed those who foretold the coming of the Righteous One, whose betrayers and murderers you have now become. [53] You received the law under the direction of angels and yet have not kept it."

GENESIS 15:13–14

[13] Then the LORD said to Abram, "Know this for certain: Your offspring will be resident aliens for four hundred years in a land that does not belong to them and will be enslaved and oppressed. [14] However, I will judge the nation they serve, and afterward they will go out with many possessions."

DEUTERONOMY 15:18

"Do not regard it as a hardship when you set him free, because he worked for you six years—worth twice the wages of a hired worker. Then the LORD your God will bless you in everything you do."

RESPONSE

Day 10

What did you notice
about this passage?

What does this teach
you about God?

How does this lead
you to pray?

How are you
challenged to
live differently?

THE EARLY CHURCH GROWS

Day 11

ACTS 7:54-60

THE FIRST CHRISTIAN MARTYR

54 When they heard these things, they were enraged and gnashed their teeth at him. 55 Stephen, full of the Holy Spirit, gazed into heaven. He saw the glory of God, and Jesus standing at the right hand of God. 56 He said, "Look, I see the heavens opened and the Son of Man standing at the right hand of God!"

57 They yelled at the top of their voices, covered their ears, and together rushed against him. 58 They dragged him out of the city and began to stone him. And the witnesses laid their garments at the feet of a young man named Saul. 59 While they were stoning Stephen, he called out:

"Lord Jesus, receive my spirit!"

60 He knelt down and cried out with a loud voice, "Lord, do not hold this sin against them!" And after saying this, he died.

SAUL THE PERSECUTOR

¹ Saul agreed with putting him to death.

On that day a severe persecution broke out against the church in Jerusalem, and all except the apostles were scattered throughout the land of Judea and Samaria. ² Devout men buried Stephen and mourned deeply over him. ³ Saul, however, was ravaging the church. He would enter house after house, drag off men and women, and put them in prison.

PHILIP IN SAMARIA

⁴ So those who were scattered went on their way preaching the word. ⁵ Philip went down to a city in Samaria and proclaimed the Messiah to them. ⁶ The crowds were all paying attention to what Philip said, as they listened and saw the signs he was performing. ⁷ For unclean spirits, crying out with a loud voice, came out of many who were possessed, and many who were paralyzed and lame were healed. ⁸ So there was great joy in that city.

THE RESPONSE OF SIMON

⁹ A man named Simon had previously practiced sorcery in that city and amazed the Samaritan people, while claiming to be somebody great. ¹⁰ They all paid attention to him, from the least of them to the greatest, and they said, "This man is called the Great Power of God." ¹¹ They were attentive to him because he had amazed them with his sorceries for a long time. ¹² But when they believed Philip, as he proclaimed the good news about the kingdom of God and the name of Jesus Christ, both men and women were baptized. ¹³ Even Simon himself believed. And after he was baptized, he followed Philip everywhere and was amazed as he observed the signs and great miracles that were being performed.

SIMON'S SIN

¹⁴ When the apostles who were at Jerusalem heard that Samaria had received the word of God, they sent Peter and John to them. ¹⁵ After they went down there, they prayed for them so the Samaritans might receive the Holy Spirit because he had not yet come down on any of them. ¹⁶ (They had only been baptized in the name of the Lord Jesus.) ¹⁷ Then Peter and John laid their hands on them, and they received the Holy Spirit.

[18] When Simon saw that the Spirit was given through the laying on of the apostles' hands, he offered them money, [19] saying, "Give me this power also so that anyone I lay hands on may receive the Holy Spirit."

[20] But Peter told him, "May your silver be destroyed with you, because you thought you could obtain the gift of God with money! [21] You have no part or share in this matter, because your heart is not right before God.

[22] Therefore repent of this wickedness of yours, and pray to the Lord that, if possible, your heart's intent may be forgiven.

[23] For I see you are poisoned by bitterness and bound by wickedness."

[24] "Pray to the Lord for me," Simon replied, "so that nothing you have said may happen to me."

[25] So, after they had testified and spoken the word of the Lord, they traveled back to Jerusalem, preaching the gospel in many villages of the Samaritans.

THE CONVERSION OF THE ETHIOPIAN OFFICIAL

[26] An angel of the Lord spoke to Philip: "Get up and go south to the road that goes down from Jerusalem to Gaza." (This is the desert road.) [27] So he got up and went. There was an Ethiopian man, a eunuch and high official of Candace, queen of the Ethiopians, who was in charge of her entire treasury. He had come to worship in Jerusalem [28] and was sitting in his chariot on his way home, reading the prophet Isaiah aloud.

[29] The Spirit told Philip, "Go and join that chariot."

[30] When Philip ran up to it, he heard him reading the prophet Isaiah, and said, "Do you understand what you're reading?"

[31] "How can I," he said, "unless someone guides me?" So he invited Philip to come up and sit with him. [32] Now the Scripture passage he was reading was this:

He was led like a sheep to the slaughter,
and as a lamb is silent before its shearer,

so he does not open his mouth.
³³ In his humiliation justice was denied him.
Who will describe his generation?
For his life is taken from the earth.

³⁴ The eunuch said to Philip, "I ask you, who is the prophet saying this about—himself or someone else?" ³⁵ Philip proceeded to tell him the good news about Jesus, beginning with that Scripture.

³⁶ As they were traveling down the road, they came to some water. The eunuch said, "Look, there's water. What would keep me from being baptized?" ³⁸ So he ordered the chariot to stop, and both Philip and the eunuch went down into the water, and he baptized him. ³⁹ When they came up out of the water, the Spirit of the Lord carried Philip away, and the eunuch did not see him any longer but went on his way rejoicing. ⁴⁰ Philip appeared in Azotus, and he was traveling and preaching the gospel in all the towns until he came to Caesarea.

2 KINGS 2:11

As they continued walking and talking, a chariot of fire with horses of fire suddenly appeared and separated the two of them. Then Elijah went up into heaven in the whirlwind.

ISAIAH 56:3-5

³ No foreigner who has joined himself to the LORD
should say,
"The LORD will exclude me from his people,"
and the eunuch should not say,
"Look, I am a dried-up tree."
⁴ For the LORD says this:
"For the eunuchs who keep my Sabbaths,
and choose what pleases me,
and hold firmly to my covenant,
⁵ I will give them, in my house and within my walls,
a memorial and a name
better than sons and daughters.
I will give each of them an everlasting name
that will never be cut off."

RESPONSE

Day 11

What did you notice
about this passage?

What does this teach
you about God?

How does this lead
you to pray?

How are you
challenged to
live differently?

The book of Acts is a narrative. Narratives don't just tell us about events; they introduce us to key people and how their lives relate to one another. This diagram shows how the key people in Acts are connected.

THEOPHILUS

The man to whom Luke dedicated the book of Acts.

ACTS 1:1

LUKE

Wrote Acts and likely interviewed Peter so he could write the Gospel of Luke. Traveled with Paul.

ACTS 1:1; LUKE 1:2; COLOSSIANS 4:14

JAMES

Jesus's half-brother who led the church in Jerusalem. Recognized Paul's conversion and affirmed his ministry to Gentiles.

ACTS 12:1–2; GALATIANS 2:9

SIMON THE MAGICIAN

Samaritan who wanted to buy from Peter and John the ability to give the Holy Spirit to another person.

ACTS 8:9–25

GAMALIEL

Pharisee and member of the Sanhedrin, the Jewish ruling council. His reasoning secured Peter and the apostles' release from prison. Taught Paul about Scripture before Paul's conversion.

ACTS 5:35; 22:3

MATTHIAS

Chosen by the apostles to replace Judas Iscariot.

ACTS 1:15–26

PETER

Disciple of Jesus. Apostle to the Jews and a leader in the Jerusalem church.

ACTS 1:12–14; 15:7

CORNELIUS

Centurion in Caesarea who invited Peter to his home. Among the first Gentiles to receive the Holy Spirit.

ACTS 10:1–48

PHILIP

Chosen by the Twelve as a deacon in the Jerusalem church. Led the Ethiopian eunuch to faith.

ACTS 6:1–7

ANANIAS AND SAPPHIRA

Lied to God and to Peter about their generosity and were struck dead.

ACTS 5:1–11

DORCAS

Also known as Tabitha. Christian woman from Joppa who died, but God used Peter to raise her back to life.

ACTS 9:36–43

STEPHEN

Deacon in the Jerusalem church with Philip. First Christian martyr, whose death was witnessed by Paul.

ACTS 6:1–15; 7:54–60

FESTUS

Judean governor who
sent Paul to Rome to
stand trial.

ACTS 25:1–12

DEMETRIUS

Silversmith who started a
riot in Ephesus because
he was angry with Paul.

ACTS 19:23–29

LYDIA

First convert to Christianity
in Asia Minor. A merchant
of purple dye.

ACTS 16:11–15

PAUL

Also known as Saul.
Temporarily blinded on
the road to Damascus.
He became a follower of
Jesus and an apostle to
the Gentiles.

ACTS 9:1–9

SILAS

Friend of Paul who traveled
with him on his second
missionary journey. Served
as Peter's secretary.

ACTS 15:40–41;
1 PETER 5:12

EUTYCHUS

Fell out of a window during
one of Paul's sermons. God
used Paul to raise him from
the dead.

ACTS 20:7–12

BARNABAS

Accompanied Paul and
John Mark on the first
missionary journey.

ACTS 9:26–30

FELIX

Judean governor who left
Paul in prison and often
visited him there.

ACTS 24:10–21

JOHN MARK

Barnabas's cousin.
Accompanied Barnabas
and Paul on their first
missionary journey. Author
of the Gospel of Mark, for
which he relied heavily on
Peter's eyewitness account.

ACTS 15:36–39

APOLLOS

Preacher known for
his eloquence. Trained
by Priscilla and Aquila.

ACTS 18:24–28

PRISCILLA
AND AQUILA

Tentmakers who befriended
Paul in Corinth and went
with him to Ephesus.

ACTS 18:1–23

THE ROAD TO DAMASCUS

Day 12

 DID YOU KNOW...

The first twelve chapters of Acts focus primarily on the ministry of Peter, while the remaining sixteen chapters focus on Paul.

ACTS 9:1-31

THE DAMASCUS ROAD

¹ Now Saul was still breathing threats and murder against the disciples of the Lord. He went to the high priest ² and requested letters from him to the synagogues in Damascus, so that if he found any men or women who belonged to the Way, he might bring them as prisoners to Jerusalem. ³ As he traveled and was nearing Damascus, a light from heaven suddenly flashed around him. ⁴ Falling to the ground, he heard a voice saying to him, "Saul, Saul, why are you persecuting me?"

⁵ "Who are you, Lord?" Saul said.

"I am Jesus, the one you are persecuting," he replied. ⁶ "But get up and go into the city, and you will be told what you must do."

⁷ The men who were traveling with him stood speechless, hearing the sound but seeing no one. ⁸ Saul got up from the ground, and though his eyes were open, he could see nothing. So they took him by the hand and led him into Damascus. ⁹ He was unable to see for three days and did not eat or drink.

[10] There was a disciple in Damascus named Ananias, and the Lord said to him in a vision, "Ananias."

"Here I am, Lord," he replied.

[11] "Get up and go to the street called Straight," the Lord said to him, "to the house of Judas, and ask for a man from Tarsus named Saul, since he is praying there. [12] In a vision he has seen a man named Ananias coming in and placing his hands on him so that he may regain his sight."

[13] "Lord," Ananias answered, "I have heard from many people about this man, how much harm he has done to your saints in Jerusalem. [14] And he has authority here from the chief priests to arrest all who call on your name."

[15] But the Lord said to him, "Go, for this man is my chosen instrument to take my name to Gentiles, kings, and Israelites. [16] I will show him how much he must suffer for my name."

[17] Ananias went and entered the house. He placed his hands on him and said, "Brother Saul, the Lord Jesus, who appeared to you on the road you were traveling, has sent me so that you may regain your sight and be filled with the Holy Spirit."

[18] At once something like scales fell from his eyes, and he regained his sight. Then he got up and was baptized. [19] And after taking some food, he regained his strength.

SAUL PROCLAIMING THE MESSIAH

Saul was with the disciples in Damascus for some time. [20] Immediately he began proclaiming Jesus in the synagogues: "He is the Son of God."

[21] All who heard him were astounded and said, "Isn't this the man in Jerusalem who was causing havoc for those who called on this name and came here for the purpose of taking them as prisoners to the chief priests?"

[22] But Saul grew stronger and kept confounding the Jews who lived in Damascus by proving that Jesus is the Messiah.

[23] After many days had passed, the Jews conspired to kill him, [24] but Saul learned of their plot. So they were watching the gates day and night intending to kill him, [25] but his disciples took him by night and lowered him in a large basket through an opening in the wall.

SAUL IN JERUSALEM

[26] When he arrived in Jerusalem, he tried to join the disciples, but they were all afraid of him, since they did not believe he was a disciple. [27] Barnabas, however, took him and brought him to the apostles and explained to them how Saul had seen the Lord on the road and that the Lord had talked to him, and how in Damascus he had spoken boldly in the name of Jesus. [28] Saul was coming and going with them in Jerusalem, speaking boldly in the name of the Lord. [29] He conversed and debated with the Hellenistic Jews, but they tried to kill him. [30] When the brothers found out, they took him down to Caesarea and sent him off to Tarsus.

THE CHURCH'S GROWTH

[31] So the church throughout all Judea, Galilee, and Samaria had peace and was strengthened. Living in the fear of the Lord and encouraged by the Holy Spirit, it increased in numbers.

PAUL DEFENDS HIS APOSTLESHIP

[11] For I want you to know, brothers and sisters, that the gospel preached by me is not of human origin.

[12] For I did not receive it from a human source and I was not taught it, but it came by a revelation of Jesus Christ.

[13] For you have heard about my former way of life in Judaism: I intensely persecuted God's church and tried to destroy it. [14] I advanced in Judaism beyond many contemporaries among my people, because I was extremely zealous for the traditions of my ancestors. [15] But when God, who from my mother's womb set me apart and called me by his grace, was pleased [16] to reveal his Son in me, so that I could preach him among the Gentiles, I did not immediately consult with anyone.

2 CORINTHIANS 3:12–13

[12] Since, then, we have such a hope, we act with great boldness. [13] We are not like Moses, who used to put a veil over his face to prevent the Israelites from gazing steadily until the end of the glory of what was being set aside…

RESPONSE

Day 12

What did you notice
about this passage?

What does this teach
you about God?

How does this lead
you to pray?

How are you
challenged to
live differently?

THEY ALL JOINED TOGETHER

In the spirit of Acts 2:42, choose a time to gather with a group to read Scripture aloud and discuss the text together. Read the account of Philip and the Ethiopian eunuch, and pray that the Holy Spirit would teach you about the character of God from His Word.

TURN TO PAGE 80 AND READ ACTS 8:26–40 TOGETHER. DISCUSS THE PASSAGE USING THE QUESTIONS PROVIDED.

CHECK OUT THE GATHERING GUIDE ON PAGE 136 FOR RECIPE AND HYMN IDEAS TO INCORPORATE INTO YOUR GROUP TIME!

QUESTIONS

1.   What do you notice about this passage?

2.   What did Philip do when he was called to go on the desert road? What can we learn about Christ's provision from Philip's decision?

3.   How was the eunuch using his time?

4.   How did the eunuch respond to instruction? How does Christ call us to respond to instruction?

PRAYER

Close your time together by praying for one another.

GRACE DAY

GRACE DAY

GRACE DAY

GRACE DAY

GRACE DAY

GRACE DAY

Seeing the depth of our sin, a painful sight though it is, brings us freedom when it compels us to confession and repentance.

Take this day as an opportunity to catch up on your reading, pray, and rest in the presence of the Lord. Pray Acts 3:19-20 for a specific person in your life and for yourself.

Therefore repent and turn back, so that your sins may be wiped out, that seasons of refreshing may come from the presence of the Lord.

ACTS 3:19–20

T   R

U

Weekly Truth

Scripture is God-breathed and true. When we
memorize it, we carry the gospel with us wherever
we go.

As we read through Acts, we are memorizing
Acts 17:24–29, a passage from Paul's eloquent yet
succinct presentation of the gospel to the Greek
philosophers at the Areopagus. By memorizing one
verse per week, we will have all six verses committed
to memory by the end of the study. This week's verse
is highlighted here.

T   H

²⁴ The God who made the world and everything in it—he is Lord of heaven and earth—does not live in shrines made by hands. ²⁵ Neither is he served by human hands, as though he needed anything, since he himself gives everyone life and breath and all things. ²⁶ From one man he has made every nationality to live over the whole earth and has determined their appointed times and the boundaries of where they live. ²⁷ He did this so that they might seek God, and perhaps they might reach out and find him, though he is not far from each one of us. ²⁸ For in him we live and move and have our being, as even some of your own poets have said, "For we are also his offspring." ²⁹ Since we are God's offspring then, we shouldn't think that the divine nature is like gold or silver or stone, an image fashioned by human art and imagination.

PETER HEALS IN CHRIST'S NAME

Day 15

ACTS 9:32-43

THE HEALING OF AENEAS

³² As Peter was traveling from place to place, he also came down to the saints who lived in Lydda. ³³ There he found a man named Aeneas, who was paralyzed and had been bedridden for eight years. ³⁴ Peter said to him,

"Aeneas, Jesus Christ heals you. Get up and make your bed,"

and immediately he got up. ³⁵ So all who lived in Lydda and Sharon saw him and turned to the Lord.

DORCAS RESTORED TO LIFE

³⁶ In Joppa there was a disciple named Tabitha (which is translated Dorcas). She was always doing good works and acts of charity. ³⁷ About that time she became sick and died. After washing her, they placed her in a room upstairs. ³⁸ Since Lydda was near Joppa, the disciples heard that Peter was there and sent two men to him who urged him, "Don't delay in coming with us." ³⁹ Peter got up and went with them. When he arrived, they led him to the room upstairs. And all the widows approached him,

weeping and showing him the robes and clothes that Dorcas had made while she was with them. [40] Peter sent them all out of the room. He knelt down, prayed, and turning toward the body said, "Tabitha, get up." She opened her eyes, saw Peter, and sat up. [41] He gave her his hand and helped her stand up. He called the saints and widows and presented her alive. [42] This became known throughout Joppa, and many believed in the Lord. [43] Peter stayed for some time in Joppa with Simon, a leather tanner.

MARK 5:21–43

A GIRL RESTORED AND A WOMAN HEALED

[21] When Jesus had crossed over again by boat to the other side, a large crowd gathered around him while he was by the sea. [22] One of the synagogue leaders, named Jairus, came, and when he saw Jesus, he fell at his feet [23] and begged him earnestly, "My little daughter is dying. Come and lay your hands on her so that she can get well and live." [24] So Jesus went with him, and a large crowd was following and pressing against him.

[25] Now a woman suffering from bleeding for twelve years [26] had endured much under many doctors. She had spent everything she had and was not helped at all. On the contrary, she became worse. [27] Having heard about Jesus, she came up behind him in the crowd and touched his clothing. [28] For she said, "If I just touch his clothes, I'll be made well." [29] Instantly her flow of blood ceased, and she sensed in her body that she was healed of her affliction.

[30] At once Jesus realized in himself that power had gone out from him. He turned around in the crowd and said, "Who touched my clothes?"

[31] His disciples said to him, "You see the crowd pressing against you, and yet you say, 'Who touched me?'"

[32] But he was looking around to see who had done this. [33] The woman, with fear and trembling, knowing what had happened to her, came and fell down before him, and told him the whole truth. [34] "Daughter," he said to her, "your faith has saved you. Go in peace and be healed from your affliction."

[35] While he was still speaking, people came from the synagogue leader's house and said, "Your daughter is dead. Why bother the teacher anymore?"

36 When Jesus overheard what was said, he told the synagogue leader, "Don't be afraid. Only believe." 37 He did not let anyone accompany him except Peter, James, and John, James's brother. 38 They came to the leader's house, and he saw a commotion—people weeping and wailing loudly. 39 He went in and said to them, "Why are you making a commotion and weeping? The child is not dead but asleep." 40 They laughed at him, but he put them all outside. He took the child's father, mother, and those who were with him, and entered the place where the child was. 41 Then he took the child by the hand and said to her, "Talitha koum" (which is translated, "Little girl, I say to you, get up"). 42 Immediately the girl got up and began to walk. (She was twelve years old.) At this they were utterly astounded. 43 Then he gave them strict orders that no one should know about this and told them to give her something to eat.

PSALM 36:8-9

8 They are filled from the abundance of your house.
You let them drink from your refreshing stream.
9 For the wellspring of life is with you.
By means of your light we see light.

RESPONSE

Day 15

What did you notice
about this passage?

What does this teach
you about God?

How does this lead
you to pray?

How are you
challenged to
live differently?

GOOD NEWS FOR THE GENTILES

Day 16

ACTS 10

CORNELIUS'S VISION

¹ There was a man in Caesarea named Cornelius, a centurion of what was called the Italian Regiment. ² He was a devout man and feared God along with his whole household. He did many charitable deeds for the Jewish people and always prayed to God. ³ About three in the afternoon he distinctly saw in a vision an angel of God who came in and said to him, "Cornelius."

⁴ Staring at him in awe, he said, "What is it, Lord?"

The angel told him, "Your prayers and your acts of charity have ascended as a memorial offering before God. ⁵ Now send men to Joppa and call for Simon, who is also named Peter. ⁶ He is lodging with Simon, a tanner, whose house is by the sea."

⁷ When the angel who spoke to him had gone, he called two of his household servants and a devout soldier, who was one of those who attended him. ⁸ After explaining everything to them, he sent them to Joppa.

[9] The next day, as they were traveling and nearing the city, Peter went up to pray on the roof about noon. [10] He became hungry and wanted to eat, but while they were preparing something, he fell into a trance. [11] He saw heaven opened and an object that resembled a large sheet coming down, being lowered by its four corners to the earth. [12] In it were all the four-footed animals and reptiles of the earth, and the birds of the sky. [13] A voice said to him, "Get up, Peter; kill and eat."

[14] "No, Lord!" Peter said. "For I have never eaten anything impure and ritually unclean."

[15] Again, a second time, the voice said to him, "What God has made clean, do not call impure." [16] This happened three times, and suddenly the object was taken up into heaven.

PETER VISITS CORNELIUS

[17] While Peter was deeply perplexed about what the vision he had seen might mean, right away the men who had been sent by Cornelius, having asked directions to Simon's house, stood at the gate. [18] They called out, asking if Simon, who was also named Peter, was lodging there.

[19] While Peter was thinking about the vision, the Spirit told him, "Three men are here looking for you. [20] Get up, go downstairs, and go with them with no doubts at all, because I have sent them."

[21] Then Peter went down to the men and said, "Here I am, the one you're looking for. What is the reason you're here?"

[22] They said, "Cornelius, a centurion, an upright and God-fearing man, who has a good reputation with the whole Jewish nation, was divinely directed by a holy angel to call you to his house and to hear a message from you." [23] Peter then invited them in and gave them lodging.

The next day he got up and set out with them, and some of the brothers from Joppa went with him. [24] The following day he entered Caesarea. Now Cornelius was expecting them and had called together his relatives and close friends. [25] When Peter entered, Cornelius met him, fell at his feet, and worshiped him.

²⁶ But Peter lifted him up and said, "Stand up. I myself am also a man." ²⁷ While talking with him, he went in and found a large gathering of people. ²⁸ Peter said to them, "You know it's forbidden for a Jewish man to associate with or visit a foreigner, but God has shown me that I must not call any person impure or unclean. ²⁹ That's why I came without any objection when I was sent for. So may I ask why you sent for me?"

³⁰ Cornelius replied, "Four days ago at this hour, at three in the afternoon, I was praying in my house. Just then a man in dazzling clothing stood before me ³¹ and said, 'Cornelius, your prayer has been heard, and your acts of charity have been remembered in God's sight. ³² Therefore send someone to Joppa and invite Simon here, who is also named Peter. He is lodging in Simon the tanner's house by the sea.' ³³ So I immediately sent for you, and it was good of you to come. So now we are all in the presence of God to hear everything you have been commanded by the Lord."

GOOD NEWS FOR GENTILES

³⁴ Peter began to speak: "Now I truly understand that God doesn't show favoritism, ³⁵ but in every nation the person who fears him and does what is right is acceptable to him. ³⁶ He sent the message to the Israelites, proclaiming the good news of peace through Jesus Christ—he is Lord of all. ³⁷ You know the events that took place throughout all Judea, beginning from Galilee after the baptism that John preached: ³⁸ how God anointed Jesus of Nazareth with the Holy Spirit and with power, and how he went about doing good and healing all who were under the tyranny of the devil, because God was with him. ³⁹ We ourselves are witnesses of everything he did in both the Judean country and in Jerusalem, and yet they killed him by hanging him on a tree. ⁴⁰ God raised up this man on the third day and caused him to be seen, ⁴¹ not by all the people, but by us whom God appointed as witnesses, who ate and drank with him after he rose from the dead. ⁴² He commanded us to preach to the people and to testify that he is the one appointed by God to be the judge of the living and the dead. ⁴³ All the prophets testify about him that through his name everyone who believes in him receives forgiveness of sins."

GENTILE CONVERSION AND BAPTISM

⁴⁴ While Peter was still speaking these words, the Holy Spirit came down on all those who heard the message. ⁴⁵ The circumcised believers who had come with Peter were amazed because the gift of the Holy Spirit had been poured out even on the Gentiles. ⁴⁶ For they heard them speaking in other tongues and declaring the greatness of God.

Then Peter responded, [47] "Can anyone withhold water and prevent these people from being baptized, who have received the Holy Spirit just as we have?" [48] He commanded them to be baptized in the name of Jesus Christ. Then they asked him to stay for a few days.

ISAIAH 52:7–10

[7] How beautiful on the mountains
are the feet of the herald,
who proclaims peace,
who brings news of good things,
who proclaims salvation,
who says to Zion, "Your God reigns!"
[8] The voices of your watchmen—
they lift up their voices,
shouting for joy together;
for every eye will see
when the LORD returns to Zion.
[9] Be joyful, rejoice together,
you ruins of Jerusalem!
For the LORD has comforted his people;
he has redeemed Jerusalem.
[10] The LORD has displayed his holy arm
in the sight of all the nations;
all the ends of the earth will see
the salvation of our God.

GALATIANS 3:13

Christ redeemed us from the curse of the law by becoming a curse for us, because it is written, Cursed is everyone who is hung on a tree.

SHE READS TRUTH | HE READS TRUTH 107

RESPONSE

Day 16

What did you notice
about this passage?

What does this teach
you about God?

How does this lead
you to pray?

How are you
challenged to
live differently?

SALVATION IS
FOR EVERYONE

Day 17

ACTS 11

GENTILE SALVATION DEFENDED

[1] The apostles and the brothers and sisters who were throughout Judea heard that the Gentiles had also received the word of God. [2] When Peter went up to Jerusalem, the circumcision party criticized him, [3] saying, "You went to uncircumcised men and ate with them."

[4] Peter began to explain to them step by step: [5] "I was in the town of Joppa praying, and I saw, in a trance, an object that resembled a large sheet coming down, being lowered by its four corners from heaven, and it came to me. [6] When I looked closely and considered it, I saw the four-footed animals of the earth, the wild beasts, the reptiles, and the birds of the sky. [7] I also heard a voice telling me, 'Get up, Peter; kill and eat.'

[8] "'No, Lord!' I said. 'For nothing impure or ritually unclean has ever entered my mouth.' [9] But a voice answered from heaven a second time, 'What God has made clean, you must not call impure.'

[10] "Now this happened three times, and everything was drawn up again into heaven. [11] At that very moment, three men who had been sent to

me from Caesarea arrived at the house where we were. [12] The Spirit told me to accompany them with no doubts at all. These six brothers also accompanied me, and we went into the man's house. [13] He reported to us how he had seen the angel standing in his house and saying, 'Send to Joppa, and call for Simon, who is also named Peter. [14] He will speak a message to you by which you and all your household will be saved.'

[15] "As I began to speak, the Holy Spirit came down on them, just as on us at the beginning. [16] I remembered the word of the Lord, how he said, 'John baptized with water, but you will be baptized with the Holy Spirit.'

[17] If, then, God gave them the same gift that he also gave to us when we believed in the Lord Jesus Christ, how could I possibly hinder God?"

[18] When they heard this they became silent. And they glorified God, saying, "So then, God has given repentance resulting in life even to the Gentiles."

THE CHURCH IN ANTIOCH

[19] Now those who had been scattered as a result of the persecution that started because of Stephen made their way as far as Phoenicia, Cyprus, and Antioch, speaking the word to no one except Jews. [20] But there were some of them, men from Cyprus and Cyrene, who came to Antioch and began speaking to the Greeks also, proclaiming the good news about the Lord Jesus. [21] The Lord's hand was with them, and a large number who believed turned to the Lord. [22] News about them reached the church in Jerusalem, and they sent out Barnabas to travel as far as Antioch. [23] When he arrived and saw the grace of God, he was glad and encouraged all of them to remain true to the Lord with devoted hearts, [24] for he was a good man, full of the Holy Spirit and of faith. And large numbers of people were added to the Lord.

[25] Then he went to Tarsus to search for Saul, [26] and when he found him he brought him to Antioch. For a whole year they met with the church and taught large numbers. The disciples were first called Christians at Antioch.

FAMINE RELIEF

[27] In those days some prophets came down from Jerusalem to Antioch. [28] One of them, named Agabus, stood up and predicted by the Spirit that

there would be a severe famine throughout the Roman world. This took place during the reign of Claudius. ²⁹ Each of the disciples, according to his ability, determined to send relief to the brothers and sisters who lived in Judea. ³⁰ They did this, sending it to the elders by means of Barnabas and Saul.

1 PETER 4:16–19

¹⁶ But if anyone suffers as a Christian, let him not be ashamed but let him glorify God in having that name. ¹⁷ For the time has come for judgment to begin with God's household, and if it begins with us, what will the outcome be for those who disobey the gospel of God?

> ¹⁸ And if a righteous person is saved with difficulty,
> what will become of the ungodly and the sinner?

¹⁹ So then, let those who suffer according to God's will entrust themselves to a faithful Creator while doing what is good.

ROMANS 15:25–28

²⁵ Right now I am traveling to Jerusalem to serve the saints, ²⁶ because Macedonia and Achaia were pleased to make a contribution for the poor among the saints in Jerusalem. ²⁷ Yes, they were pleased, and indeed are indebted to them. For if the Gentiles have shared in their spiritual benefits, then they are obligated to minister to them in material needs. ²⁸ So when I have finished this and safely delivered the funds to them, I will visit you on the way to Spain.

RESPONSE

Day 17

What did you notice
about this passage?

What does this teach
you about God?

How does this lead
you to pray?

How are you
challenged to
live differently?

ACTS IN HISTORY

B

AD 33

Crucifixion, resurrection, and ascension of Jesus*

The Holy Spirit comes at Pentecost

KEY

B BIBLICAL EVENT

E EXTRABIBLICAL EVENT

ROMAN EMPEROR

B

AD 34

Stephen martyred

Paul converted on the road to Damascus

EMPEROR TIBERIUS

AD 14–37

EMPEROR CALIGULA

AD 37–41

10   **20**   **30**   **40**

Though the dates in this timeline have been carefully researched, scholars disagree on the precise year of Jesus's birth and the duration of His ministry prior to His crucifixion.

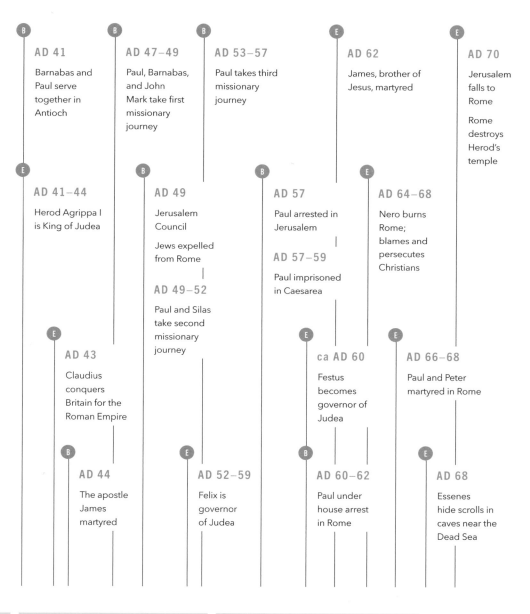

AD 41

Barnabas and Paul serve together in Antioch

AD 47–49

Paul, Barnabas, and John Mark take first missionary journey

AD 53–57

Paul takes third missionary journey

AD 62

James, brother of Jesus, martyred

AD 70

Jerusalem falls to Rome

Rome destroys Herod's temple

AD 41–44

Herod Agrippa I is King of Judea

AD 49

Jerusalem Council

Jews expelled from Rome

AD 49–52

Paul and Silas take second missionary journey

AD 57

Paul arrested in Jerusalem

AD 57–59

Paul imprisoned in Caesarea

AD 64–68

Nero burns Rome; blames and persecutes Christians

AD 43

Claudius conquers Britain for the Roman Empire

ca AD 60

Festus becomes governor of Judea

AD 66–68

Paul and Peter martyred in Rome

AD 44

The apostle James martyred

AD 52–59

Felix is governor of Judea

AD 60–62

Paul under house arrest in Rome

AD 68

Essenes hide scrolls in caves near the Dead Sea

EMPEROR CLAUDIUS

AD 41–54

EMPEROR NERO

AD 54–68

50   60   70

PETER RESCUED BY AN ANGEL

Day 18

ACTS 12

JAMES MARTYRED AND PETER JAILED

[1] About that time King Herod violently attacked some who belonged to the church, [2] and he executed James, John's brother, with the sword. [3] When he saw that it pleased the Jews, he proceeded to arrest Peter too, during the Festival of Unleavened Bread. [4] After the arrest, he put him in prison and assigned four squads of four soldiers each to guard him, intending to bring him out to the people after the Passover. [5] So Peter was kept in prison, but the church was praying fervently to God for him.

PETER RESCUED

[6] When Herod was about to bring him out for trial, that very night Peter, bound with two chains, was sleeping between two soldiers, while the sentries in front of the door guarded the prison. [7] Suddenly an angel of the Lord appeared, and a light shone in the cell. Striking Peter on the side, he woke him up and said, "Quick, get up!" And the chains fell off his wrists. [8] "Get dressed," the angel told him, "and put on your sandals." And he did. "Wrap your cloak around you," he told him, "and follow me." [9] So he went out and followed, and he did not know that what the angel did was really happening, but he thought he was seeing a vision.

¹⁰ After they passed the first and second guards, they came to the iron gate that leads into the city, which opened to them by itself. They went outside and passed one street, and suddenly the angel left him.

¹¹ When Peter came to himself, he said, "Now I know for certain that the Lord has sent his angel and rescued me from Herod's grasp and from all that the Jewish people expected." ¹² As soon as he realized this, he went to the house of Mary, the mother of John Mark, where many had assembled and were praying. ¹³ He knocked at the door of the outer gate, and a servant named Rhoda came to answer. ¹⁴ She recognized Peter's voice, and because of her joy, she did not open the gate but ran in and announced that Peter was standing at the outer gate.

¹⁵ "You're out of your mind!" they told her. But she kept insisting that it was true, and they said, "It's his angel." ¹⁶ Peter, however, kept on knocking, and when they opened the door and saw him, they were amazed.

¹⁷ Motioning to them with his hand to be silent, he described to them how the Lord had brought him out of the prison. "Tell these things to James and the brothers," he said, and he left and went to another place.

¹⁸ At daylight, there was a great commotion among the soldiers as to what had become of Peter. ¹⁹ After Herod had searched and did not find him, he interrogated the guards and ordered their execution. Then Herod went down from Judea to Caesarea and stayed there.

HEROD'S DEATH

²⁰ Herod had been very angry with the people of Tyre and Sidon. Together they presented themselves before him. After winning over Blastus, who was in charge of the king's bedroom, they asked for peace, because their country was supplied with food from the king's country. ²¹ On an appointed day, dressed in royal robes and seated on the throne, Herod delivered a speech to them. ²² The assembled people began to shout, "It's the voice of a god and not of a man!" ²³ At once an angel of the Lord struck him because he did not give the glory to God, and he was eaten by worms and died.

²⁴ But the word of God flourished and multiplied. ²⁵ After they had completed their relief mission, Barnabas and Saul returned to Jerusalem, taking along John who was called Mark.

SUFFERING AND SERVICE

[35] James and John, the sons of Zebedee, approached him and said, "Teacher, we want you to do whatever we ask you."

[36] "What do you want me to do for you?" he asked them.

[37] They answered him, "Allow us to sit at your right and at your left in your glory."

[38] Jesus said to them, "You don't know what you're asking. Are you able to drink the cup I drink or to be baptized with the baptism I am baptized with?"

[39] "We are able," they told him.

Jesus said to them, "You will drink the cup I drink, and you will be baptized with the baptism I am baptized with. [40] But to sit at my right or left is not mine to give; instead, it is for those for whom it has been prepared."

ISAIAH 42:8

"I am the LORD. That is my name,
and I will not give my glory to another
or my praise to idols."

RESPONSE

Day 18

What did you notice
about this passage?

What does this teach
you about God?

How does this lead
you to pray?

How are you
challenged to
live differently?

PAUL'S FIRST MISSIONARY JOURNEY

Day 19

ACTS 13

PREPARING FOR THE MISSION FIELD

[1] Now in the church at Antioch there were prophets and teachers: Barnabas, Simeon who was called Niger, Lucius of Cyrene, Manaen, a close friend of Herod the tetrarch, and Saul.

[2] As they were worshiping the Lord and fasting, the Holy Spirit said, "Set apart for me Barnabas and Saul for the work to which I have called them." [3] Then after they had fasted, prayed, and laid hands on them, they sent them off.

THE MISSION TO CYPRUS

[4] So being sent out by the Holy Spirit, they went down to Seleucia, and from there they sailed to Cyprus. [5] Arriving in Salamis, they proclaimed the word of God in the Jewish synagogues. They also had John as their assistant. [6] When they had traveled the whole island as far as Paphos, they came across a sorcerer, a Jewish false prophet named Bar-Jesus. [7] He was with the proconsul, Sergius Paulus, an intelligent man. This man summoned Barnabas and Saul and wanted to hear the word of God.

[8] But Elymas the sorcerer (that is the meaning of his name) opposed them and tried to turn the proconsul away from the faith.

[9] But Saul—also called Paul—filled with the Holy Spirit, stared straight at Elymas [10] and said, "You are full of all kinds of deceit and trickery, you son of the devil and enemy of all that is right. Won't you ever stop perverting the straight paths of the Lord? [11] Now, look, the Lord's hand is against you. You are going to be blind, and will not see the sun for a time." Immediately a mist and darkness fell on him, and he went around seeking someone to lead him by the hand.

[12] Then, when he saw what happened, the proconsul believed, because he was astonished at the teaching of the Lord.

PAUL'S SERMON IN ANTIOCH OF PISIDIA

[13] Paul and his companions set sail from Paphos and came to Perga in Pamphylia, but John left them and went back to Jerusalem. [14] They continued their journey from Perga and reached Pisidian Antioch. On the Sabbath day they went into the synagogue and sat down. [15] After the reading of the Law and the Prophets, the leaders of the synagogue sent word to them, saying, "Brothers, if you have any word of encouragement for the people, you can speak."

[16] Paul stood up and motioned with his hand and said: "Fellow Israelites, and you who fear God, listen! [17] The God of this people Israel chose our ancestors, made the people prosper during their stay in the land of Egypt, and led them out of it with a mighty arm. [18] And for about forty years he put up with them in the wilderness; [19] and after destroying seven nations in the land of Canaan, he gave them their land as an inheritance. [20] This all took about 450 years. After this, he gave them judges until Samuel the prophet. [21] Then they asked for a king, and God gave them Saul the son of Kish, a man of the tribe of Benjamin, for forty years. [22] After removing him, he raised up David as their king and testified about him:' I have found David the son of Jesse to be a man after my own heart, who will carry out all my will.'

[23] "From this man's descendants, as he promised, God brought to Israel the Savior, Jesus.

²⁴ Before his coming to public attention, John had previously proclaimed a baptism of repentance to all the people of Israel. ²⁵ Now as John was completing his mission, he said, 'Who do you think I am? I am not the one. But one is coming after me, and I am not worthy to untie the sandals on his feet.'

²⁶ "Brothers and sisters, children of Abraham's race, and those among you who fear God, it is to us that the word of this salvation has been sent. ²⁷ Since the residents of Jerusalem and their rulers did not recognize him or the sayings of the prophets that are read every Sabbath, they have fulfilled their words by condemning him. ²⁸ Though they found no grounds for the death sentence, they asked Pilate to have him killed. ²⁹ When they had carried out all that had been written about him, they took him down from the tree and put him in a tomb. ³⁰ But God raised him from the dead, ³¹ and he appeared for many days to those who came up with him from Galilee to Jerusalem, who are now his witnesses to the people. ³² And we ourselves proclaim to you the good news of the promise that was made to our ancestors. ³³ God has fulfilled this for us, their children, by raising up Jesus, as it is written in the second Psalm:

You are my Son;
today I have become your Father.

³⁴ As to his raising him from the dead, never to return to decay, he has spoken in this way, I will give you the holy and sure promises of David. ³⁵ Therefore he also says in another passage, You will not let your Holy One see decay. ³⁶ For David, after serving God's purpose in his own generation, fell asleep, was buried with his fathers, and decayed, ³⁷ but the one God raised up did not decay. ³⁸ Therefore, let it be known to you, brothers and sisters, that through this man forgiveness of sins is being proclaimed to you. ³⁹ Everyone who believes is justified through him from everything that you could not be justified from through the law of Moses. ⁴⁰ So beware that what is said in the prophets does not happen to you:

⁴¹ Look, you scoffers,
marvel and vanish away,
because I am doing a work in your days,
a work that you will never believe,
even if someone were to explain it to you."

PAUL AND BARNABAS IN ANTIOCH

⁴² As they were leaving, the people urged them to speak about these matters the following Sabbath. ⁴³ After the synagogue had been dismissed, many of the Jews and devout converts to Judaism followed Paul and Barnabas, who were speaking with them and urging them to continue in the grace of God.

⁴⁴ The following Sabbath almost the whole town assembled to hear the word of the Lord. ⁴⁵ But when the Jews saw the crowds, they were filled with jealousy and began to contradict what Paul was saying, insulting him.

⁴⁶ Paul and Barnabas boldly replied, "It was necessary that the word of God be spoken to you first. Since you reject it and judge yourselves unworthy of eternal life, we are turning to the Gentiles. ⁴⁷ For this is what the Lord has commanded us:

I have made you
a light for the Gentiles
to bring salvation
to the end of the earth."

[48] When the Gentiles heard this, they rejoiced and honored the word of the Lord, and all who had been appointed to eternal life believed. [49] The word of the Lord spread through the whole region. [50] But the Jews incited the prominent God-fearing women and the leading men of the city. They stirred up persecution against Paul and Barnabas and expelled them from their district. [51] But Paul and Barnabas shook the dust off their feet against them and went to Iconium. [52] And the disciples were filled with joy and the Holy Spirit.

GALATIANS 3:10–14

LAW AND PROMISE

[10] For all who rely on the works of the law are under a curse, because it is written, Everyone who does not do everything written in the book of the law is cursed. [11] Now it is clear that no one is justified before God by the law, because the righteous will live by faith. [12] But the law is not based on faith; instead, the one who does these things will live by them. [13] Christ redeemed us from the curse of the law by becoming a curse for us, because it is written, Cursed is everyone who is hung on a tree. [14] The purpose was that the blessing of Abraham would come to the Gentiles by Christ Jesus, so that we could receive the promised Spirit through faith.

ISAIAH 49:6

He says,
"It is not enough for you to be my servant
raising up the tribes of Jacob
and restoring the protected ones of Israel.
I will also make you a light for the nations,
to be my salvation to the ends of the earth."

RESPONSE

Day 19

What did you notice
about this passage?

What does this teach
you about God?

How does this lead
you to pray?

How are you
challenged to
live differently?

Week 3

THEY ALL JOINED TOGETHER

In the spirit of Acts 2:42, choose a time to gather with a group to read Scripture aloud and discuss the text together. Acts 12:5-19 is about Peter's imprisonment and how believers in Jerusalem faithfully gathered together in the name of Christ to pray. Read the account, and pray that the Holy Spirit would teach you about the character of God from His Word.

TURN TO PAGE 119 AND READ ACTS 12:5–19 TOGETHER. DISCUSS THE PASSAGE USING THE QUESTIONS PROVIDED.

CHECK OUT THE GATHERING GUIDE ON PAGE 136 FOR RECIPE AND HYMN IDEAS TO INCORPORATE INTO YOUR GROUP TIME!

QUESTIONS

1. What do you notice about this passage?

2. Bound and sleeping between two soldiers, Peter's imprisonment seemed secure. It would have been impossible for him to even cough without attracting notice. What was the church's response to this?

3. Was Peter's deliverance an answer to prayer? What do we learn here about the power of prayer?

4. Do we need to fear when it seems like enemies surround us? Read Psalm 27:3 and discuss.

5. How did the believers who had gathered to pray respond when Peter showed up at their door? Why do you think this was the case? How would you react if an answer to your prayer walked into your group's gathering today?

PRAYER

Close your time together by praying for one another.

GRACE DAY

GRACE DAY

DAY 20
WEEK 3

GRACE DAY

GRACE DAY

GRACE DAY

GRACE DAY

We give thanks to God for the gift of baptism.

Take this day as an opportunity to catch up on your reading, pray, and rest in the presence of the Lord. Pray Acts 8:36 for a specific person in your life and for yourself.

As they were traveling down the road, they came to some water. The eunuch said, "Look, there's water. What would keep me from being baptized?"

ACTS 8:36

T

R

U

Weekly Truth

Scripture is God-breathed and true. When we memorize it, we carry the gospel with us wherever we go.

As we read through Acts, we are memorizing Acts 17:24–29, a passage from Paul's eloquent yet succinct presentation of the gospel to the Greek philosophers at the Areopagus. By memorizing one verse per week, we will have all six verses committed to memory by the end of the study. This week's verse is highlighted here.

T

H

²⁴ The God who made the world and everything in it—he is Lord of heaven and earth—does not live in shrines made by hands. ²⁵ Neither is he served by human hands, as though he needed anything, since he himself gives everyone life and breath and all things. ²⁶ From one man he has made every nationality to live over the whole earth and has determined their appointed times and the boundaries of where they live. ²⁷ He did this so that they might seek God, and perhaps they might reach out and find him, though he is not far from each one of us. ²⁸ For in him we live and move and have our being, as even some of your own poets have said, "For we are also his offspring." ²⁹ Since we are God's offspring then, we shouldn't think that the divine nature is like gold or silver or stone, an image fashioned by human art and imagination.

SHE READS TRUTH | HE READS TRUTH   135

THEY DEVOTED
THEMSELVES TO
THE APOSTLES'
TEACHING, TO
THE FELLOWSHIP,
TO THE BREAKING
OF BREAD, AND
TO PRAYER.

ACTS 2:42

The book of Acts tells us that believers in the early Church devoted themselves to fellowship together—they met regularly in their homes to eat and pray. As you meet with your group, take a look through the recipes and hymns included in this gathering guide for ideas to incorporate into your time together.

HYMNS

138 CLASSIC BRUSCHETTA

RASPBERRY CREAMSICLES **142**

BBQ PINEAPPLE CHICKEN **144**

140

MINTY SUMMER SALAD

146

MEXICAN STREET CORN

Recipe

CLASSIC BRUSCHETTA

SERVES

INGREDIENTS

1 baguette

¼ cup olive oil

6 Roma tomatoes, diced

½ red onion, chopped

1 tablespoon garlic, minced

½ cup fresh basil, chopped

2 tablespoons balsamic vinegar

4 tablespoons parmesan cheese

Salt and pepper, to taste

DIRECTIONS

1. Preheat oven to 400°F. Slice baguette and brush with olive oil. Turn down the oven to 350°F, and toast the baguette slices for 5 minutes.

2. Combine the tomatoes, onion, garlic, basil, olive oil, and vinegar in a large bowl.

3. Top each toasted baguette piece with the bruschetta mixture. Finish with a sprinkling of parmesan cheese and salt and pepper.

TO SAVE TIME, MAKE THE BRUCHETTA MIXTURE IN ADVANCE.

Recipe

MINTY SUMMER SALAD

SERVES **6**

INGREDIENTS

1 pint strawberries, sliced

1 cantaloupe, diced

¼ cup balsamic vinegar

Fresh mint, sliced or whole

Cracked black pepper

DIRECTIONS

1. Toss fruit in a bowl with balsamic vinegar and mint leaves.

2. Garnish generously with black pepper. (It seems scary, but trust us—this is the best part.)

3. Chill for an hour and serve cold.

DON'T SKIP THE MINT FOR COLOR AND FLAVOR!

Recipe

RASPBERRY CREAMSICLES

SERVES **6**

INGREDIENTS

8 oz fresh or frozen raspberries

Juice of 1 lime, freshly squeezed

1 tablespoon sugar

32 oz vanilla yogurt

½ cup + 2 tablespoons canned coconut milk

Salt

DIRECTIONS

1. Combine raspberries, lime juice, and sugar in a medium bowl. Smash with fork and set aside.

2. In separate bowl, combine yogurt, coconut milk, and a pinch of salt. Gently add berry mixture to yogurt mixture, being careful not to overmix—the streaks are part of the charm!

3. Pour mixture into popsicle molds, insert the sticks, and freeze overnight until solid. If you have trouble freeing them from their molds, run the container under hot water.

SERVE ON ICE WITH A LAST-MINUTE SQUEEZE OF LIME JUICE.

Recipe

BBQ PINEAPPLE CHICKEN

SERVES

INGREDIENTS

4 boneless, skinless chicken breasts

1 pound bacon

1 fresh pineapple or 1 can pineapple chunks

1 red onion

1–2 green or red peppers

2 cups white rice

1 cup pineapple preserves

1 cup hickory-smoke barbecue sauce

DIRECTIONS

1. Soak 8 bamboo skewers or use 8 long metal skewers. Trim excess fat from chicken and cut into 1- to 2-inch cubes. Cut bacon strips into halves and wrap around chicken cubes. Cut pineapple, onion, and peppers into uniform sizes.

2. Thread skewers in this order: red onion, chicken wrapped in bacon, pineapple, and pepper, repeating until all ingredients are used.

3. Prepare grill with medium-hot coals or heat gas grill to medium-high. Place skewers on grill and cook 6 minutes; turn and grill 6 more minutes until chicken is cooked through.

4. Prepare rice according to instructions.

5. Stir barbecue sauce and pineapple preserves together in a 1:1 ratio and warm on stovetop.

6. Remove skewers from grill. Brush with warm sauce. Serve over rice, with extra sauce on the side.

ASSEMBLE SKEWERS IN ADVANCE AND STORE IN FRIDGE FOR A QUICK MEAL!

Recipe

MEXICAN STREET CORN

SERVES

INGREDIENTS

12 ears of corn

½ cup feta cheese

1 tablespoon garlic salt

1 tablespoon chili powder

½ cup mayonnaise

Bunch of cilantro leaves

2 limes, juiced

DIRECTIONS

1. Carefully shuck corn, removing as much of the silk as you can. Then grill or blanch. If you grill, aim to fully cook the kernels before they start to char. If you blanch, keep them rolling in boiling water for about five minutes, just until the kernels get tender.

2. Meanwhile, combine feta, garlic salt, chili powder, mayonnaise, cilantro, and lime juice.

3. Spoon mixture over cooked corn and serve.

A CLASSIC SUMMERTIME CROWD PLEASER.

Hymn

HOW FIRM A FOUNDATION

TEXT

ROBERT KEENE, 1787

TUNE

AMERICAN FOLK MELODY

How firm a foundation, you saints of the Lord,
is laid for your faith in His excellent Word!
What more can He say than to you He has said,
to you who for refuge to Jesus have fled?

"Fear not, I am with you, O be not dismayed,
for I am your God, and will still give you aid;
I'll strengthen you, help you, and cause you
    to stand,
upheld by My righteous, omnipotent hand.

"When through the deep waters I call you to go,
the rivers of sorrow shall not overflow;
for I will be with you, your troubles to bless,
and sanctify to you your deepest distress.

"When through fiery trials your pathway shall lie,
My grace, all-sufficient, shall be your supply;
the flame shall not hurt you, I only design
your dross to consume and your gold to refine.

"The soul that on Jesus has leaned for repose,
I will not, I will not desert to its foes;
that soul, though all hell should endeavor
    to shake,
I'll never, no never, no never forsake!"

Hymn

COME, THOU FOUNT OF EVERY BLESSING

TEXT

ROBERT ROBINSON, 1758

TUNE

NETTLETON

Come, Thou fount of every blessing,
tune my heart to sing Thy grace;
streams of mercy, never ceasing,
call for songs of loudest praise.
Teach me some melodious sonnet,
sung by flaming tongues above.
Praise the mount—I'm fixed upon it
mount of God's redeeming love.

Here I find my greatest treasure;
hither by Thy help I've come;
and I hope, by Thy good pleasure,
safely to arrive at home.
Jesus sought me when a stranger,
wandering from the fold of God;
He, to rescue me from danger,
bought me with His precious blood.

Oh, to grace how great a debtor
daily I'm constrained to be!
Let Thy goodness, like a fetter,
bind my wandering heart to Thee:
prone to wander, Lord, I feel it,
prone to leave the God I love;
here's my heart, O take and seal it;
seal it for Thy courts above.

Hymn

AMAZING GRACE

TEXT

ST. 1–4, JOHN NEWTON, 1779;
ST. 5, ANONYMOUS, ca 1790

TUNE

VIRGINIA HARMONY, 1831;
ARR. EDWIN O. EXCELL, 1851–1921

Amazing grace! How sweet the sound,
That saved a wretch like me!
I once was lost, but now am found,
Was blind, but now I see.

'Twas grace that taught my heart to fear,
And grace my fears relieved;
How precious did that grace appear
The hour I first believed!

The Lord has promised good to me,
His Word my hope secures;
He will my shield and portion be
As long as life endures.

Through many dangers, toils and snares,
I have already come;
'Tis grace has brought me safe thus far,
And grace will lead me home.

When we've been there ten thousand years,
Bright shining as the sun,
We've no less days to sing God's praise
Than when we'd first begun.

	G		G	D⁷	Em	C
1	A - maz - ing____ grace!	How	sweet		the
2	'Twas grace that___ taught	my	heart		to
3	The Lord has___ prom - ised	good		to
4	Through man - y____ dan - gers,	toils		and
5	When we've been __ there ten	thou - sand

	G		G		G	D⁷(sus4)
	sound,	That	saved	a____ wretch	like	me!____
	fear,	And	grace	my___ fears	re -	lieved;____
	me,	His	Word	my___ hope	se -	cures;____
	snares,	I	have	al - read - y	come;____
	years,	Bright	shin - ing___	as	the	sun,____

	D⁷		G		G⁷		C
	___	I	once____ was__	lost,	but	now____	am
	___	How	pre - cious did	that	grace____	ap -
	___	He	will____ my__ shield	and	por -	tion __
	___	'Tis	grace____ hath _ brought	me	safe____	thus _
	___	We've	no ____ less__ days	to	sing____	God's

	G	Em	G/D	D⁷	G
	found,	Was blind,	but __ now	I	see. ____
	pear	The hour	I____ first	be -	lieved!____
	be	As long	as___ life	en -	dures. ____
	far,	And grace	will__ lead	me	home. ____
	praise	Than when	we'd_ first	be -	gun. ____

GROWTH AND PERSECUTION IN ICONIUM

Day 22

ACTS 14

GROWTH AND PERSECUTION IN ICONIUM

¹ In Iconium they entered the Jewish synagogue, as usual, and spoke in such a way that a great number of both Jews and Greeks believed. ² But the unbelieving Jews stirred up the Gentiles and poisoned their minds against the brothers. ³ So they stayed there a long time and spoke boldly for the Lord, who testified to the message of his grace by enabling them to do signs and wonders. ⁴ But the people of the city were divided, some siding with the Jews and others with the apostles. ⁵ When an attempt was made by both the Gentiles and Jews, with their rulers, to mistreat and stone them, ⁶ they found out about it and fled to the Lycaonian towns of Lystra and Derbe and to the surrounding countryside. ⁷ There they continued preaching the gospel.

MISTAKEN FOR GODS IN LYSTRA

⁸ In Lystra a man was sitting who was without strength in his feet, had never walked, and had been lame from birth. ⁹ He listened as Paul spoke. After looking directly at him and seeing that he had faith to be healed, ¹⁰ Paul said in a loud voice, "Stand up on your feet!" And he jumped up and began to walk around.

[11] When the crowds saw what Paul had done, they shouted, saying in the Lycaonian language, "The gods have come down to us in human form!" [12] Barnabas they called Zeus, and Paul, Hermes, because he was the chief speaker. [13] The priest of Zeus, whose temple was just outside the town, brought bulls and wreaths to the gates because he intended, with the crowds, to offer sacrifice.

[14] The apostles Barnabas and Paul tore their robes when they heard this and rushed into the crowd, shouting: [15] "People! Why are you doing these things? We are people also, just like you, and we are proclaiming good news to you, that you turn from these worthless things to the living God, who made the heaven, the earth, the sea, and everything in them. [16] In past generations he allowed all the nations to go their own way, [17] although he did not leave himself without a witness, since he did what is good by giving you rain from heaven and fruitful seasons and filling you with food and your hearts with joy." [18] Even though they said these things, they barely stopped the crowds from sacrificing to them.

[19] Some Jews came from Antioch and Iconium, and when they won over the crowds, they stoned Paul and dragged him out of the city, thinking he was dead. [20] After the disciples gathered around him, he got up and went into the town. The next day he left with Barnabas for Derbe.

CHURCH PLANTING

[21] After they had preached the gospel in that town and made many disciples, they returned to Lystra, to Iconium, and to Antioch, [22] strengthening the disciples by encouraging them to continue in the faith and by telling them, "It is necessary to go through many hardships to enter the kingdom of God." [23] When they had appointed elders for them in every church and prayed with fasting, they committed them to the Lord in whom they had believed.

[24] They passed through Pisidia and came to Pamphylia. [25] After they had spoken the word in Perga, they went down to Attalia. [26] From there they sailed back to Antioch where they had been commended to the grace of God for the work they had now completed. [27] After they arrived and gathered the church together, they reported everything God had done with them and that he had opened the door of faith to the Gentiles. [28] And they spent a considerable time with the disciples.

STRUGGLES IN THE CHRISTIAN LIFE

[10] But you have followed my teaching, conduct, purpose, faith, patience, love, and endurance, [11] along with the persecutions and sufferings that came to me in Antioch, Iconium, and Lystra. What persecutions I endured—and yet the Lord rescued me from them all. [12] In fact, all who want to live a godly life in Christ Jesus will be persecuted.

COLOSSIANS 4:2-4

SPEAKING TO GOD AND OTHERS

[2] Devote yourselves to prayer; stay alert in it with thanksgiving. [3] At the same time, pray also for us that God may open a door to us for the word, to speak the mystery of Christ, for which I am in chains, [4] so that I may make it known as I should.

RESPONSE

Day 22

What did you notice
about this passage?

What does this teach
you about God?

How does this lead
you to pray?

How are you
challenged to
live differently?

IS CHRIST ENOUGH?

Day 23

ACTS 15:1–35

DISPUTE IN ANTIOCH

¹ Some men came down from Judea and began to teach the brothers: "Unless you are circumcised according to the custom prescribed by Moses, you cannot be saved." ² After Paul and Barnabas had engaged them in serious argument and debate, Paul and Barnabas and some others were appointed to go up to the apostles and elders in Jerusalem about this issue. ³ When they had been sent on their way by the church, they passed through both Phoenicia and Samaria, describing in detail the conversion of the Gentiles, and they brought great joy to all the brothers and sisters.

⁴ When they arrived at Jerusalem, they were welcomed by the church, the apostles, and the elders, and they reported all that God had done with them. ⁵ But some of the believers who belonged to the party of the Pharisees stood up and said, "It is necessary to circumcise them and to command them to keep the law of Moses."

⁶ The apostles and the elders gathered to consider this matter. ⁷ After there had been much debate, Peter stood up and said to them: "Brothers and sisters, you are aware that in the early days God made a choice among you, that by my mouth the Gentiles would hear the gospel message and believe. ⁸ And God, who knows the heart, bore witness to them by giving them the Holy Spirit, just as he also did to us.

⁹ He made no distinction between us and them, cleansing their hearts by faith.

¹⁰ Now then, why are you testing God by putting a yoke on the disciples' necks that neither our ancestors nor we have been able to bear? ¹¹ On the contrary, we believe that we are saved through the grace of the Lord Jesus in the same way they are."

¹² The whole assembly became silent and listened to Barnabas and Paul describe all the signs and wonders God had done through them among the Gentiles. ¹³ After they stopped speaking, James responded: "Brothers and sisters, listen to me. ¹⁴ Simeon has reported how God first intervened to take from the Gentiles a people for his name. ¹⁵ And the words of the prophets agree with this, as it is written:

¹⁶ After these things I will return
and rebuild David's fallen tent.
I will rebuild its ruins
and set it up again,
¹⁷ so the rest of humanity
may seek the Lord—
even all the Gentiles
who are called by my name—
declares the Lord
who makes these things ¹⁸ known from long ago.

¹⁹ Therefore, in my judgment, we should not cause difficulties for those among the Gentiles who turn to God, ²⁰ but instead we should write to them to abstain from things polluted by idols, from sexual immorality, from eating anything that has been strangled, and from blood. ²¹ For since ancient times, Moses has had those who proclaim him in every city, and every Sabbath day he is read aloud in the synagogues."

²² Then the apostles and the elders, with the whole church, decided to select men who were among them and to send them to Antioch with Paul and Barnabas: Judas, called Barsabbas, and Silas, both leading men among the brothers. ²³ They wrote:

"From the apostles and the elders, your brothers,

To the brothers and sisters among the Gentiles in Antioch, Syria, and Cilicia:

Greetings.

²⁴ Since we have heard that some without our authorization went out from us and troubled you with their words and unsettled your hearts, ²⁵ we have unanimously decided to select men and send them to you along with our dearly loved Barnabas and Paul, ²⁶ who have risked their lives for the name of our Lord Jesus Christ. ²⁷ Therefore we have sent Judas and Silas, who will personally report the same things by word of mouth. ²⁸ For it was the Holy Spirit's decision—and ours— not to place further burdens on you beyond these requirements: ²⁹ that you abstain from food offered to idols, from blood, from eating anything that has been strangled, and from sexual immorality. You will do well if you keep yourselves from these things.

Farewell."

THE OUTCOME OF THE JERUSALEM LETTER

³⁰ So they were sent off and went down to Antioch, and after gathering the assembly, they delivered the letter. ³¹ When they read it, they rejoiced because of its encouragement. ³² Both Judas and Silas, who were also prophets themselves, encouraged the brothers and sisters and strengthened them with a long message. ³³ After spending some time there, they were sent back in peace by the brothers and sisters to those who had sent them. ³⁵ But Paul and Barnabas, along with many others, remained in Antioch, teaching and proclaiming the word of the Lord.

JEWISH VIOLATION OF THE LAW

[17] Now if you call yourself a Jew, and rely on the law, and boast in God, [18] and know his will, and approve the things that are superior, being instructed from the law, [19] and if you are convinced that you are a guide for the blind, a light to those in darkness, [20] an instructor of the ignorant, a teacher of the immature, having the embodiment of knowledge and truth in the law— [21] you then, who teach another, don't you teach yourself? You who preach, "You must not steal"—do you steal? [22] You who say, "You must not commit adultery"—do you commit adultery? You who detest idols, do you rob their temples? [23] You who boast in the law, do you dishonor God by breaking the law? [24] For, as it is written: The name of God is blasphemed among the Gentiles because of you.

GALATIANS 5:1

For freedom, Christ set us free. Stand firm then and don't submit again to a yoke of slavery.

RESPONSE

Day 23

What did you notice
about this passage?

What does this teach
you about God?

How does this lead
you to pray?

How are you
challenged to
live differently?

START OF THE SECOND MISSIONARY JOURNEY

Day 24

ACTS 15:36–41

PAUL AND BARNABAS PART COMPANY

[36] After some time had passed, Paul said to Barnabas, "Let's go back and visit the brothers and sisters in every town where we have preached the word of the Lord and see how they're doing." [37] Barnabas wanted to take along John Mark. [38] But Paul insisted that they should not take along this man who had deserted them in Pamphylia and had not gone on with them to the work. [39] They had such a sharp disagreement that they parted company, and Barnabas took Mark with him and sailed off to Cyprus. [40] But Paul chose Silas and departed, after being commended by the brothers and sisters to the grace of the Lord. [41] He traveled through Syria and Cilicia, strengthening the churches.

ACTS 16:1–15

PAUL SELECTS TIMOTHY

[1] Paul went on to Derbe and Lystra, where there was a disciple named Timothy, the son of a believing Jewish woman, but his father was a Greek. [2] The brothers and sisters at Lystra and Iconium spoke highly

of him. ³ Paul wanted Timothy to go with him; so he took him and circumcised him because of the Jews who were in those places, since they all knew that his father was a Greek. ⁴ As they traveled through the towns, they delivered the decisions reached by the apostles and elders at Jerusalem for the people to observe.

⁵ So the churches were strengthened in the faith and grew daily in numbers.

EVANGELIZATION OF EUROPE

⁶ They went through the region of Phrygia and Galatia; they had been forbidden by the Holy Spirit to speak the word in Asia. ⁷ When they came to Mysia, they tried to go into Bithynia, but the Spirit of Jesus did not allow them. ⁸ Passing by Mysia they went down to Troas. ⁹ During the night Paul had a vision in which a Macedonian man was standing and pleading with him, "Cross over to Macedonia and help us!" ¹⁰ After he had seen the vision, we immediately made efforts to set out for Macedonia, concluding that God had called us to preach the gospel to them.

LYDIA'S CONVERSION

¹¹ From Troas we put out to sea and sailed straight for Samothrace, the next day to Neapolis, ¹² and from there to Philippi, a Roman colony and a leading city of the district of Macedonia. We stayed in that city for several days. ¹³ On the Sabbath day we went outside the city gate by the river, where we expected to find a place of prayer. We sat down and spoke to the women gathered there. ¹⁴ A God-fearing woman named Lydia, a dealer in purple cloth from the city of Thyatira, was listening. The Lord opened her heart to respond to what Paul was saying. ¹⁵ After she and her household were baptized, she urged us, "If you consider me a believer in the Lord, come and stay at my house." And she persuaded us.

JOHN 15:26

"When the Counselor comes, the one I will send to you from the Father —the Spirit of truth who proceeds from the Father—he will testify about me."

[19] Although I am free from all and not anyone's slave, I have made myself a slave to everyone, in order to win more people. [20] To the Jews I became like a Jew, to win Jews; to those under the law, like one under the law—though I myself am not under the law—to win those under the law. [21] To those who are without the law, like one without the law—though I am not without God's law but under the law of Christ—to win those without the law.

RESPONSE

Day 24

What did you notice
about this passage?

What does this teach
you about God?

How does this lead
you to pray?

How are you
challenged to
live differently?

MACEDONIA

Adriatic Sea

ROME

THREE TAVERNS
FORUM OF APPIUS

PUTEOLI

ITALY

AMPHIPOL
PHILIPPI

THESSALONICA

NEAPOL

BEREA

SAMOTHRAC

APOLLONIA

ACHAIA

ATHENS

CORINTH

CENCHREAE

RHEGIUM

SICILY

SYRACUSE

MALTA

Mediterranean Sea

CRETE

FAIR HAVENS

0 MI   100   200
N
0 KM   100   200   300   400

PAUL'S MISSIONARY JOURNEYS

The book of Acts begins with Jesus telling His disciples to share the gospel with people "in Jerusalem, in all Judea and Samaria, and to the end of the earth" (1:8). It was Paul and his friends who first took on the challenge of traveling to far-off places to tell people about Jesus. On this map, you can see the places Paul visited, bringing good news to people from every walk of life.

	ANTIOCH		SALAMIS	
FIRST JOURNEY		SELEUCIA		PAPHOS

	ANTIOCH		LYSTRA	
SECOND JOURNEY		DERBE		TROAS

	ANTIOCH		CORINTH	
THIRD JOURNEY		EPHESUS		PHILIPPI

	JERUSALEM		SIDON	
VOYAGE TO ROME		CAESAREA		MYRA

Black Sea

GALATIA

CAPPADOCIA

TROAS
ASSOS
MITYLENE

ASIA
MINOR

○— PISIDIAN ANTIOCH

○— ICONIUM

LYSTRA

DERBE

TARSUS

CHIOS
SAMOS
EPHESUS

MILETUS

CNIDUS

PERGA
ATTALIA

PAMPHYLIA

ANTIOCH
SELEUCIA

COS
RHODES

PATARA

MYRA

CYPRUS

SALAMIS

PAPHOS

SIDON

TYRE
PTOLEMAIS

CAESAREA

SAMARIA

JERUSALEM

JUDEA

PERGA — PISIDIAN ANTIOCH — ICONIUM — LYSTRA — DERBE — LYSTRA — ICONIUM — PISIDIAN ANTIOCH — PERGA — ATTALIA — ANTIOCH

AMOTHRACE — NEAPOLIS — PHILIPPI — AMPHIPOLIS — APOLLONIA — THESSALONICA — BEREA — ATHENS — CORINTH — CENCHREAE — EPHESUS — CAESAREA — JERUSALEM — ANTIOCH

TROAS — ASSOS — MITYLENE — CHIOS — SAMOS — MILETUS — COS — RHODES — PATARA — TYRE — PTOLEMAIS — CAESAREA — JERUSALEM

CNIDUS — FAIR HAVENS — MALTA — SYRACUSE — RHEGIUM — PUTEOLI — FORUM OF APPIUS — THREE TAVERNS — ROME

CONVERSION OF THE PHILIPPIAN JAILER

Day 25

ACTS 16:16–40

PAUL AND SILAS IN PRISON

[16] Once, as we were on our way to prayer, a slave girl met us who had a spirit by which she predicted the future. She made a large profit for her owners by fortune-telling. [17] As she followed Paul and us she cried out, "These men, who are proclaiming to you the way of salvation, are the servants of the Most High God." [18] She did this for many days.

Paul was greatly annoyed. Turning to the spirit, he said, "I command you in the name of Jesus Christ to come out of her!" And it came out right away.

[19] When her owners realized that their hope of profit was gone, they seized Paul and Silas and dragged them into the marketplace to the authorities. [20] Bringing them before the chief magistrates, they said, "These men are seriously disturbing our city. They are Jews [21] and are promoting customs that are not legal for us as Romans to adopt or practice." [22] The crowd joined in the attack against them, and the chief magistrates stripped off their clothes and ordered them to be beaten with rods. [23] After they had severely flogged them, they threw them in jail, ordering the jailer to

guard them carefully. [24] Receiving such an order, he put them into the inner prison and secured their feet in the stocks.

A MIDNIGHT DELIVERANCE

[25] About midnight Paul and Silas were praying and singing hymns to God, and the prisoners were listening to them. [26] Suddenly there was such a violent earthquake that the foundations of the jail were shaken, and immediately all the doors were opened, and everyone's chains came loose. [27] When the jailer woke up and saw the doors of the prison standing open, he drew his sword and was going to kill himself, since he thought the prisoners had escaped.

[28] But Paul called out in a loud voice, "Don't harm yourself, because we're all here!"

[29] The jailer called for lights, rushed in, and fell down trembling before Paul and Silas. [30] He escorted them out and said, "Sirs, what must I do to be saved?"

[31] They said, "Believe in the Lord Jesus, and you will be saved—you and your household." [32] And they spoke the word of the Lord to him along with everyone in his house. [33] He took them the same hour of the night and washed their wounds. Right away he and all his family were baptized. [34] He brought them into his house, set a meal before them, and rejoiced because he had come to believe in God with his entire household.

AN OFFICIAL APOLOGY

[35] When daylight came, the chief magistrates sent the police to say, "Release those men."

[36] The jailer reported these words to Paul: "The magistrates have sent orders for you to be released. So come out now and go in peace."

[37] But Paul said to them, "They beat us in public without a trial, although we are Roman citizens, and threw us in jail. And now are they going to send us away secretly? Certainly not! On the contrary, let them come themselves and escort us out."

[38] The police reported these words to the magistrates. They were afraid when they heard that Paul and Silas were Roman citizens. [39] So they came to appease them, and escorting them from prison, they urged them

to leave town. [40] After leaving the jail, they came to Lydia's house, where they saw and encouraged the brothers and sisters, and departed.

2 CORINTHIANS 10:3-4

[3] For although we live in the flesh, we do not wage war according to the flesh, [4] since the weapons of our warfare are not of the flesh, but are powerful through God for the demolition of strongholds...

1 PETER 2:19-21

[19] For it brings favor if, because of a consciousness of God, someone endures grief from suffering unjustly. [20] For what credit is there if when you do wrong and are beaten, you endure it? But when you do what is good and suffer, if you endure it, this brings favor with God.

[21] For you were called to this, because Christ also suffered for you, leaving you an example, that you should follow in his steps.

RESPONSE

Day 25

What did you notice
about this passage?

What does this teach
you about God?

How does this lead
you to pray?

How are you
challenged to
live differently?

PAUL PREACHES AT THE AREOPAGUS

Day 26

ACTS 17

A SHORT MINISTRY IN THESSALONICA

¹ After they passed through Amphipolis and Apollonia, they came to Thessalonica, where there was a Jewish synagogue. ² As usual, Paul went into the synagogue, and on three Sabbath days reasoned with them from the Scriptures, ³ explaining and proving that it was necessary for the Messiah to suffer and rise from the dead:

> "This Jesus I am proclaiming to you is the Messiah."

⁴ Some of them were persuaded and joined Paul and Silas, including a large number of God-fearing Greeks, as well as a number of the leading women.

RIOT IN THE CITY

⁵ But the Jews became jealous, and they brought together some wicked men from the marketplace, formed a mob, and started a riot in the city. Attacking Jason's house, they searched for them to bring them out to the

public assembly. ⁶ When they did not find them, they dragged Jason and some of the brothers before the city officials, shouting, "These men who have turned the world upside down have come here too, ⁷ and Jason has welcomed them. They are all acting contrary to Caesar's decrees, saying that there is another king—Jesus." ⁸ The crowd and city officials who heard these things were upset. ⁹ After taking a security bond from Jason and the others, they released them.

THE BEREANS SEARCH THE SCRIPTURES

¹⁰ As soon as it was night, the brothers and sisters sent Paul and Silas away to Berea. Upon arrival, they went into the synagogue of the Jews. ¹¹ The people here were of more noble character than those in Thessalonica, since they received the word with eagerness and examined the Scriptures daily to see if these things were so. ¹² Consequently, many of them believed, including a number of the prominent Greek women as well as men. ¹³ But when the Jews from Thessalonica found out that the word of God had been proclaimed by Paul at Berea, they came there too, agitating and upsetting the crowds. ¹⁴ Then the brothers and sisters immediately sent Paul away to go to the coast, but Silas and Timothy stayed on there. ¹⁵ Those who escorted Paul brought him as far as Athens, and after receiving instructions for Silas and Timothy to come to him as quickly as possible, they departed.

PAUL IN ATHENS

¹⁶ While Paul was waiting for them in Athens, he was deeply distressed when he saw that the city was full of idols. ¹⁷ So he reasoned in the synagogue with the Jews and with those who worshiped God, as well as in the marketplace every day with those who happened to be there. ¹⁸ Some of the Epicurean and Stoic philosophers also debated with him. Some said, "What is this ignorant show-off trying to say?"

Others replied, "He seems to be a preacher of foreign deities"—because he was telling the good news about Jesus and the resurrection.

¹⁹ They took him and brought him to the Areopagus, and said, "May we learn about this new teaching you are presenting? ²⁰ Because what you say sounds strange to us, and we want to know what these things mean." ²¹ Now all the Athenians and the foreigners residing there spent their time on nothing else but telling or hearing something new.

THE AREOPAGUS ADDRESS

[22] Paul stood in the middle of the Areopagus and said: "People of Athens! I see that you are extremely religious in every respect. [23] For as I was passing through and observing the objects of your worship, I even found an altar on which was inscribed: 'To an Unknown God.' Therefore, what you worship in ignorance, this I proclaim to you. [24] The God who made the world and everything in it—he is Lord of heaven and earth—does not live in shrines made by hands. [25] Neither is he served by human hands, as though he needed anything, since he himself gives everyone life and breath and all things. [26] From one man he has made every nationality to live over the whole earth and has determined their appointed times and the boundaries of where they live. [27] He did this so that they might seek God, and perhaps they might reach out and find him, though he is not far from each one of us. [28] For in him we live and move and have our being, as even some of your own poets have said, 'For we are also his offspring.' [29] Since we are God's offspring then, we shouldn't think that the divine nature is like gold or silver or stone, an image fashioned by human art and imagination.

[30] "Therefore, having overlooked the times of ignorance, God now commands all people everywhere to repent, [31] because he has set a day when he is going to judge the world in righteousness by the man he has appointed. He has provided proof of this to everyone by raising him from the dead."

[32] When they heard about the resurrection of the dead, some began to ridicule him, but others said, "We'd like to hear from you again about this." [33] So Paul left their presence. [34] However, some people joined him and believed, including Dionysius the Areopagite, a woman named Damaris, and others with them.

ZECHARIAH 12:10

"Then I will pour out a spirit of grace and prayer on the house of David and the residents of Jerusalem, and they will look at me whom they pierced. They will mourn for him as one mourns for an only child and weep bitterly for him as one weeps for a firstborn."

THE RIGHTEOUSNESS OF GOD THROUGH FAITH

²¹ But now, apart from the law, the righteousness of God has been revealed, attested by the Law and the Prophets. ²² The righteousness of God is through faith in Jesus Christ to all who believe, since there is no distinction. ²³ For all have sinned and fall short of the glory of God. ²⁴ They are justified freely by his grace through the redemption that is in Christ Jesus. ²⁵ God presented him as an atoning sacrifice in his blood, received through faith, to demonstrate his righteousness, because in his restraint God passed over the sins previously committed. ²⁶ God presented him to demonstrate his righteousness at the present time, so that he would be righteous and declare righteous the one who has faith in Jesus.

RESPONSE

Day 26

What did you notice
about this passage?

What does this teach
you about God?

How does this lead
you to pray?

How are you
challenged to
live differently?

THEY ALL JOINED TOGETHER

In the spirit of Acts 2:42, choose a time to gather with a group to read Scripture aloud and discuss the text together. Read this account of Paul receiving a call to share the gospel in Macedonia. Pray that the Holy Spirit would teach you about the character of God from His Word.

TURN TO PAGE 167 AND READ ACTS 16:1–15 TOGETHER. DISCUSS THE PASSAGE USING THE QUESTIONS PROVIDED.

CHECK OUT THE GATHERING GUIDE ON PAGE 136 FOR RECIPE AND HYMN IDEAS TO INCORPORATE INTO YOUR GROUP TIME!

QUESTIONS

1. What do you notice about this passage?

2. Why might sharing the gospel with Romans and other Gentiles have been difficult for early Christians?

3. How did Paul and Timothy know what God wanted them to do? What can we learn about being sensitive to the Holy Spirit from this passage?

4. Once Lydia became a Christian, she immediately began looking for a way to contribute to the spread of the gospel. She invited Paul and his friends to stay with her while they ministered in Macedonia. What are some practical ways you can support the work of gospel ministry?

PRAYER

Close your time together by praying for one another.

GRACE DAY

GRACE DAY

GRACE DAY

DAY 27

WEEK 4

GRACE DAY

GRACE DAY

GRACE DAY

Take this day as an opportunity to catch up on your reading, pray, and rest in the presence of the Lord.

Connect with the members of your family and community in prayer as you pray Acts 13:38-39 for them and yourself.

³⁸ Therefore, let it be known to you, brothers and sisters, that through this man forgiveness of sins is being proclaimed to you. ³⁹ Everyone who believes is justified through him from everything that you could not be justified from through the law of Moses.

ACTS 13:38–39

T R

U

T H

Weekly Truth

Scripture is God-breathed and true. When we memorize it, we carry the gospel with us wherever we go.

As we read through Acts, we are memorizing Acts 17:24–29, a passage from Paul's eloquent yet succinct presentation of the gospel to the Greek philosophers at the Areopagus. By memorizing one verse per week, we will have all six verses committed to memory by the end of the study. This week's verse is highlighted here.

²⁴ The God who made the world and everything in it—he is Lord of heaven and earth—does not live in shrines made by hands. ²⁵ Neither is he served by human hands, as though he needed anything, since he himself gives everyone life and breath and all things. ²⁶ From one man he has made every nationality to live over the whole earth and has determined their appointed times and the boundaries of where they live. ²⁷ He did this so that they might seek God, and perhaps they might reach out and find him, though he is not far from each one of us. ²⁸ For in him we live and move and have our being, as even some of your own poets have said, "For we are also his offspring." ²⁹ Since we are God's offspring then, we shouldn't think that the divine nature is like gold or silver or stone, an image fashioned by human art and imagination.

PAUL'S SECOND MISSIONARY JOURNEY ENDS

Day 29

ACTS 18

FOUNDING THE CORINTHIAN CHURCH

¹ After this, he left Athens and went to Corinth, ² where he found a Jew named Aquila, a native of Pontus, who had recently come from Italy with his wife Priscilla because Claudius had ordered all the Jews to leave Rome. Paul came to them, ³ and since they were of the same occupation, tentmakers by trade, he stayed with them and worked. ⁴ He reasoned in the synagogue every Sabbath and tried to persuade both Jews and Greeks.

⁵ When Silas and Timothy arrived from Macedonia, Paul devoted himself to preaching the word and testified to the Jews that Jesus is the Messiah. ⁶ When they resisted and blasphemed, he shook out his clothes and told them, "Your blood is on your own heads! I am innocent. From now on I will go to the Gentiles." ⁷ So he left there and went to the house of a man named Titius Justus, a worshiper of God, whose house was next door to the synagogue. ⁸ Crispus, the leader of the synagogue, believed in the Lord, along with his whole household. Many of the Corinthians, when they heard, believed and were baptized.

⁹ The Lord said to Paul in a night vision, "Don't be afraid, but keep on speaking and don't be silent. ¹⁰ For I am with you, and no one will lay a hand on you to hurt you, because I have many people in this city." ¹¹ He stayed there a year and a half, teaching the word of God among them.

¹² While Gallio was proconsul of Achaia, the Jews made a united attack against Paul and brought him to the tribunal. ¹³ "This man," they said, "is persuading people to worship God in ways contrary to the law."

¹⁴ As Paul was about to open his mouth, Gallio said to the Jews, "If it were a matter of wrongdoing or of a serious crime, it would be reasonable for me to put up with you Jews. ¹⁵ But if these are questions about words, names, and your own law, see to it yourselves. I refuse to be a judge of such things." ¹⁶ So he drove them from the tribunal. ¹⁷ And they all seized Sosthenes, the leader of the synagogue, and beat him in front of the tribunal, but none of these things mattered to Gallio.

THE RETURN TRIP TO ANTIOCH

¹⁸ After staying for some time, Paul said farewell to the brothers and sisters and sailed away to Syria, accompanied by Priscilla and Aquila. He shaved his head at Cenchreae because of a vow he had taken. ¹⁹ When they reached Ephesus he left them there, but he himself entered the synagogue and debated with the Jews. ²⁰ When they asked him to stay for a longer time, he declined, ²¹ but he said farewell and added, "I'll come back to you again, if God wills." Then he set sail from Ephesus.

²² On landing at Caesarea, he went up to Jerusalem and greeted the church, then went down to Antioch.

²³ After spending some time there, he set out, traveling through one place after another in the region of Galatia and Phrygia, strengthening all the disciples.

THE ELOQUENT APOLLOS

²⁴ Now a Jew named Apollos, a native Alexandrian, an eloquent man who was competent in the use of the Scriptures, arrived in Ephesus. ²⁵ He had been instructed in the way of the Lord; and being fervent in spirit, he was speaking and teaching accurately about Jesus, although he knew only John's baptism. ²⁶ He began to speak boldly in the synagogue. After Priscilla and Aquila heard him, they took him aside and explained the way of God to him more accurately. ²⁷ When he wanted to cross over to

Achaia, the brothers and sisters wrote to the disciples to welcome him. After he arrived, he was a great help to those who by grace had believed. [28] For he vigorously refuted the Jews in public, demonstrating through the Scriptures that Jesus is the Messiah.

JAMES 4:13–15

OUR WILL AND GOD'S WILL

[13] Come now, you who say, "Today or tomorrow we will travel to such and such a city and spend a year there and do business and make a profit." [14] Yet you do not know what tomorrow will bring—what your life will be! For you are like vapor that appears for a little while, then vanishes.

[15] Instead, you should say, "If the Lord wills, we will live and do this or that."

ISAIAH 51:1–2

SALVATION FOR ZION

[1] Listen to me, you who pursue righteousness,
you who seek the LORD:
Look to the rock from which you were cut,
and to the quarry from which you were dug.
[2] Look to Abraham your father,
and to Sarah who gave birth to you.
When I called him, he was only one;
I blessed him and made him many.

RESPONSE

Day 29

What did you notice
about this passage?

What does this teach
you about God?

How does this lead
you to pray?

How are you
challenged to
live differently?

PAUL'S THIRD MISSIONARY JOURNEY

Day 30

ACTS 19

TWELVE DISCIPLES OF JOHN THE BAPTIST

[1] While Apollos was in Corinth, Paul traveled through the interior regions and came to Ephesus. He found some disciples [2] and asked them, "Did you receive the Holy Spirit when you believed?"

"No," they told him, "we haven't even heard that there is a Holy Spirit."

[3] "Into what then were you baptized?" he asked them.

"Into John's baptism," they replied.

[4] Paul said, "John baptized with a baptism of repentance, telling the people that they should believe in the one who would come after him, that is, in Jesus."

[5] When they heard this, they were baptized into the name of the Lord Jesus. [6] And when Paul had laid his hands on them, the Holy Spirit came on them, and they began to speak in other tongues and to prophesy. [7] Now there were about twelve men in all.

[8] Paul entered the synagogue and spoke boldly over a period of three months, arguing and persuading them about the kingdom of God. [9] But when some became hardened and would not believe, slandering the Way in front of the crowd, he withdrew from them, taking the disciples, and conducted discussions every day in the lecture hall of Tyrannus. [10] This went on for two years, so that all the residents of Asia, both Jews and Greeks, heard the word of the Lord.

DEMONISM DEFEATED AT EPHESUS

[11] God was performing extraordinary miracles by Paul's hands, [12] so that even facecloths or aprons that had touched his skin were brought to the sick, and the diseases left them, and the evil spirits came out of them.

[13] Now some of the itinerant Jewish exorcists also attempted to pronounce the name of the Lord Jesus over those who had evil spirits, saying, "I command you by the Jesus that Paul preaches!" [14] Seven sons of Sceva, a Jewish high priest, were doing this. [15] The evil spirit answered them,

"I know Jesus, and I recognize Paul— but who are you?"

[16] Then the man who had the evil spirit jumped on them, overpowered them all, and prevailed against them, so that they ran out of that house naked and wounded. [17] When this became known to everyone who lived in Ephesus, both Jews and Greeks, they became afraid, and the name of the Lord Jesus was held in high esteem.

[18] And many who had become believers came confessing and disclosing their practices, [19] while many of those who had practiced magic collected their books and burned them in front of everyone. So they calculated their value and found it to be fifty thousand pieces of silver. [20] In this way the word of the Lord flourished and prevailed.

THE RIOT IN EPHESUS

[21] After these events, Paul resolved by the Spirit to pass through Macedonia and Achaia and go to Jerusalem. "After I've been there," he said, "It is necessary for me to see Rome as well." [22] After sending to Macedonia two of those who assisted him, Timothy and Erastus, he himself stayed in Asia for a while.

23 About that time there was a major disturbance about the Way. 24 For a person named Demetrius, a silversmith who made silver shrines of Artemis, provided a great deal of business for the craftsmen. 25 When he had assembled them, as well as the workers engaged in this type of business, he said: "Men, you know that our prosperity is derived from this business. 26 You see and hear that not only in Ephesus, but in almost all of Asia, this man Paul has persuaded and misled a considerable number of people by saying that gods made by hand are not gods. 27 Not only do we run a risk that our business may be discredited, but also that the temple of the great goddess Artemis may be despised and her magnificence come to the verge of ruin—the very one all of Asia and the world worship."

28 When they had heard this, they were filled with rage and began to cry out, "Great is Artemis of the Ephesians!" 29 So the city was filled with confusion, and they rushed all together into the amphitheater, dragging along Gaius and Aristarchus, Macedonians who were Paul's traveling companions. 30 Although Paul wanted to go in before the people, the disciples did not let him. 31 Even some of the provincial officials of Asia, who were his friends, sent word to him, pleading with him not to venture into the amphitheater. 32 Some were shouting one thing and some another, because the assembly was in confusion, and most of them did not know why they had come together. 33 Some Jews in the crowd gave instructions to Alexander after they pushed him to the front. Motioning with his hand, Alexander wanted to make his defense to the people. 34 But when they recognized that he was a Jew, they all shouted in unison for about two hours: "Great is Artemis of the Ephesians!"

35 When the city clerk had calmed the crowd down, he said, "People of Ephesus! What person is there who doesn't know that the city of the Ephesians is the temple guardian of the great Artemis, and of the image that fell from heaven? 36 Therefore, since these things are undeniable, you must keep calm and not do anything rash. 37 For you have brought these men here who are not temple robbers or blasphemers of our goddess. 38 So if Demetrius and the craftsmen who are with him have a case against anyone, the courts are in session, and there are proconsuls. Let them bring charges against one another. 39 But if you seek anything further, it must be decided in a legal assembly. 40 In fact, we run a risk of being charged with rioting for what happened today, since there is no justification that we can give as a reason for this disturbance." 41 After saying this, he dismissed the assembly.

John answered them all, "I baptize you with water, but one who is more powerful than I am is coming. I am not worthy to untie the strap of his sandals. He will baptize you with the Holy Spirit and fire."

EPHESIANS 6:12

For our struggle is not against flesh and blood, but against the rulers, against the authorities, against the cosmic powers of this darkness, against evil, spiritual forces in the heavens.

RESPONSE

Day 30

What did you notice
about this passage?

What does this teach
you about God?

How does this lead
you to pray?

How are you
challenged to
live differently?

PAUL SAYS GOODBYE TO THE EPHESIANS

Day 31

ACTS 20

PAUL IN MACEDONIA

¹ After the uproar was over, Paul sent for the disciples, encouraged them, and after saying farewell, departed to go to Macedonia. ² And when he had passed through those areas and offered them many words of encouragement, he came to Greece ³ and stayed three months. The Jews plotted against him when he was about to set sail for Syria, and so he decided to go back through Macedonia. ⁴ He was accompanied by Sopater son of Pyrrhus from Berea, Aristarchus and Secundus from Thessalonica, Gaius from Derbe, Timothy, and Tychicus and Trophimus from the province of Asia. ⁵ These men went on ahead and waited for us in Troas, ⁶ but we sailed away from Philippi after the Festival of Unleavened Bread. In five days we reached them at Troas, where we spent seven days.

EUTYCHUS REVIVED AT TROAS

⁷ On the first day of the week, we assembled to break bread. Paul spoke to them, and since he was about to depart the next day, he kept on talking until midnight. ⁸ There were many lamps in the room upstairs where we were assembled, ⁹ and a young man named Eutychus was sitting on a window sill and sank into a deep sleep as Paul kept on talking. When he

was overcome by sleep, he fell down from the third story and was picked up dead. [10] But Paul went down, bent over him, embraced him, and said, "Don't be alarmed, because he's alive." [11] After going upstairs, breaking the bread, and eating, Paul talked a long time until dawn. Then he left. [12] They brought the boy home alive and were greatly comforted.

FROM TROAS TO MILETUS

[13] We went on ahead to the ship and sailed for Assos, where we were going to take Paul on board, because these were his instructions, since he himself was going by land. [14] When he met us at Assos, we took him on board and went on to Mitylene. [15] Sailing from there, the next day we arrived off Chios. The following day we crossed over to Samos, and the day after, we came to Miletus. [16] For Paul had decided to sail past Ephesus to avoid spending time in the province of Asia, because he was hurrying to be in Jerusalem, if possible, for the day of Pentecost.

FAREWELL ADDRESS TO THE EPHESIAN ELDERS

[17] Now from Miletus, he sent to Ephesus and summoned the elders of the church. [18] When they came to him, he said to them: "You know, from the first day I set foot in Asia, how I was with you the whole time, [19] serving the Lord with all humility, with tears, and during the trials that came to me through the plots of the Jews. [20] You know that I did not avoid proclaiming to you anything that was profitable or from teaching you publicly and from house to house. [21] I testified to both Jews and Greeks about repentance toward God and faith in our Lord Jesus.

[22] "And now I am on my way to Jerusalem, compelled by the Spirit, not knowing what I will encounter there, [23] except that in every town the Holy Spirit warns me that chains and afflictions are waiting for me. [24] But I consider my life of no value to myself; my purpose is to finish my course and the ministry I received from the Lord Jesus, to testify to the gospel of God's grace.

[25] "And now I know that none of you, among whom I went about preaching the kingdom, will ever see me again. [26] Therefore I declare to you this day that I am innocent of the blood of all of you, [27] because I did not avoid declaring to you the whole plan of God. [28] Be on guard for yourselves and for all the flock of which the Holy Spirit has appointed you as overseers, to shepherd the church of God, which he purchased with his own blood. [29] I know that after my departure savage wolves

will come in among you, not sparing the flock. [30] Men will rise up even from your own number and distort the truth to lure the disciples into following them. [31] Therefore be on the alert, remembering that night and day for three years I never stopped warning each one of you with tears.

[32] "And now I commit you to God and to the word of his grace, which is able to build you up and to give you an inheritance among all who are sanctified. [33] I have not coveted anyone's silver or gold or clothing. [34] You yourselves know that I worked with my own hands to support myself and those who are with me. [35] In every way I've shown you that it is necessary to help the weak by laboring like this and to remember the words of the Lord Jesus, because he said, 'It is more blessed to give than to receive.'"

[36] After he said this, he knelt down and prayed with all of them. [37] There were many tears shed by everyone. They embraced Paul and kissed him, [38] grieving most of all over his statement that they would never see his face again. And they accompanied him to the ship.

1 CORINTHIANS 16:1–4

COLLECTION FOR THE JERUSALEM CHURCH

[1] Now about the collection for the saints: Do the same as I instructed the Galatian churches. [2] On the first day of the week, each of you is to set something aside and save in keeping with how he is prospering, so that no collections will need to be made when I come. [3] When I arrive, I will send with letters those you recommend to carry your gift to Jerusalem. [4] If it is suitable for me to go as well, they will travel with me.

PHILIPPIANS 1:20–21

[20] My eager expectation and hope is that I will not be ashamed about anything, but that now as always, with all courage, Christ will be highly honored in my body, whether by life or by death.

LIVING IS CHRIST

[21] For me, to live is Christ and to die is gain.

RESPONSE

Day 31

1

What did you notice
about this passage?

2

What does this teach
you about God?

3

How does this lead
you to pray?

4

How are you
challenged to
live differently?

PARALLELS IN LUKE AND ACTS

Acts continues the story of "all that Jesus *began* to do and teach" (Ac 1:1; emphasis added). In other words, the entire book of Acts is still Jesus's story. He's there on every page, His Spirit at work in and through His followers. Because this is the case, and because Luke is a master storyteller, themes in Luke's Gospel often resurface in the book of Acts. Most notable are the parallels between Jesus, Peter, and Paul. The following highlights some of the most visible connections.

JESUS

THE BOOK OF LUKE

 The Holy Spirit descends upon Jesus.

LK 3:21–22

 Jesus declares Old Testament scriptures have been fulfilled.

LK 4:16–27; 24:45–47

 Jesus heals with unexpected power.

LK 4:40; 5:17; 8:46

PETER

THE BOOK OF ACTS

 The Holy Spirit descends upon Peter and the disciples gathered in the upper room.

AC 2:1–4

 Peter declares Old Testament scriptures have been fulfilled.

AC 2:14–40

 Peter heals with unexpected power.

AC 5:14–16

PAUL

THE BOOK OF ACTS

Paul declares Old Testament scriptures have been fulfilled.

AC 28:23–28

Paul heals with unexpected power.

AC 19:11–12

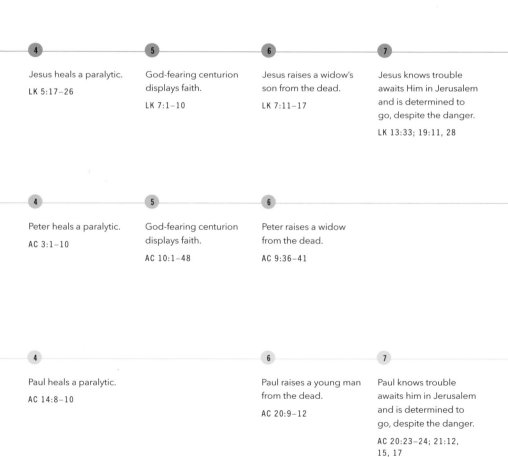

4 Jesus heals a paralytic.
LK 5:17–26

5 God-fearing centurion displays faith.
LK 7:1–10

6 Jesus raises a widow's son from the dead.
LK 7:11–17

7 Jesus knows trouble awaits Him in Jerusalem and is determined to go, despite the danger.
LK 13:33; 19:11, 28

4 Peter heals a paralytic.
AC 3:1–10

5 God-fearing centurion displays faith.
AC 10:1–48

6 Peter raises a widow from the dead.
AC 9:36–41

4 Paul heals a paralytic.
AC 14:8–10

6 Paul raises a young man from the dead.
AC 20:9–12

7 Paul knows trouble awaits him in Jerusalem and is determined to go, despite the danger.
AC 20:23–24; 21:12, 15, 17

8

Jesus enters the temple
and cleanses it.

LK 19:45–47

9

Sadducees reject
the resurrection.

LK 20:27–39

10

Jesus is brought before
the Sanhedrin.

LK 22:66–71

10

Peter and John are brought
before the Sanhedrin.

AC 4:5–22

8

Paul enters the temple and
is accused of defiling it.

AC 21:26

9

Sadducees reject
the resurrection.

AC 23:6–9

10

Paul is brought before
the Sanhedrin.

AC 22:30–23:10

11

Centurion recognizes Jesus's innocence before God.

LK 23:47

 12

Jesus is struck by the high priest's aides.

LK 22:63–64

 13

Jesus has four hearings— once before the Sanhedrin, twice before a Roman governor, and once before Herod Antipas—and is declared innocent.

LK 22:66–23:25

 11

Centurion recognizes Paul's innocence before God.

AC 27:31–32, 43

 12

Paul is struck by the high priest's aides.

AC 23:2

 13

Paul has four hearings–once before the Sanhedrin, twice before Roman governors, and once before Herod Agrippa II–and is declared innocent.

AC 22:30–26:32

PAUL GOES TO JERUSALEM

Day 32

ACTS 21:1–36

WARNINGS ON THE JOURNEY TO JERUSALEM

[1] After we tore ourselves away from them, we set sail straight for Cos, the next day to Rhodes, and from there to Patara. [2] Finding a ship crossing over to Phoenicia, we boarded and set sail. [3] After we sighted Cyprus, passing to the south of it, we sailed on to Syria and arrived at Tyre, since the ship was to unload its cargo there. [4] We sought out the disciples and stayed there seven days. Through the Spirit they told Paul not to go to Jerusalem. [5] When our time had come to an end, we left to continue our journey, while all of them, with their wives and children, accompanied us out of the city. After kneeling down on the beach to pray, [6] we said farewell to one another and boarded the ship, and they returned home.

[7] When we completed our voyage from Tyre, we reached Ptolemais, where we greeted the brothers and sisters and stayed with them for a day. [8] The next day we left and came to Caesarea, where we entered the house of Philip the evangelist, who was one of the Seven, and stayed with him. [9] This man had four virgin daughters who prophesied.

[10] After we had been there for several days, a prophet named Agabus came down from Judea. [11] He came to us, took Paul's belt, tied his own feet and hands, and said, "This is what the Holy Spirit says: 'In this way the Jews in Jerusalem will bind the man who owns this belt and deliver him over to the Gentiles.'" [12] When we heard this, both we and the local people pleaded with him not to go up to Jerusalem.

[13] Then Paul replied,

"What are you doing, weeping and breaking my heart? For I am ready not only to be bound but also to die in Jerusalem for the name of the Lord Jesus."

[14] Since he would not be persuaded, we said no more except, "The Lord's will be done."

CONFLICT OVER THE GENTILE MISSION

[15] After this we got ready and went up to Jerusalem. [16] Some of the disciples from Caesarea also went with us and brought us to Mnason of Cyprus, an early disciple, with whom we were to stay.

[17] When we reached Jerusalem, the brothers and sisters welcomed us warmly. [18] The following day Paul went in with us to James, and all the elders were present. [19] After greeting them, he reported in detail what God had done among the Gentiles through his ministry.

[20] When they heard it, they glorified God and said, "You see, brother, how many thousands of Jews there are who have believed, and they are all zealous for the law. [21] But they have been informed about you—that you are teaching all the Jews who are among the Gentiles to abandon Moses, telling them not to circumcise their children or to live according to our customs. [22] So what is to be done? They will certainly hear that you've come. [23] Therefore do what we tell you: We have four men who have made a vow. [24] Take these men, purify yourself along with them, and pay for them to get their heads shaved. Then everyone will know that what they were told about you amounts to nothing, but that you yourself are also careful about observing the law. [25] With regard to the Gentiles who have believed, we have written a letter containing our decision that they

should keep themselves from food sacrificed to idols, from blood, from what is strangled, and from sexual immorality."

THE RIOT IN THE TEMPLE

[26] So the next day, Paul took the men, having purified himself along with them, and entered the temple, announcing the completion of the purification days when the offering would be made for each of them. [27] When the seven days were nearly over, some Jews from the province of Asia saw him in the temple, stirred up the whole crowd, and seized him, [28] shouting, "Fellow Israelites, help! This is the man who teaches everyone everywhere against our people, our law, and this place. What's more, he also brought Greeks into the temple and has defiled this holy place." [29] For they had previously seen Trophimus the Ephesian in the city with him, and they supposed that Paul had brought him into the temple.

[30] The whole city was stirred up, and the people rushed together. They seized Paul, dragged him out of the temple, and at once the gates were shut.

[31] As they were trying to kill him, word went up to the commander of the regiment that all Jerusalem was in chaos. [32] Taking along soldiers and centurions, he immediately ran down to them. Seeing the commander and the soldiers, they stopped beating Paul. [33] Then the commander approached, took him into custody, and ordered him to be bound with two chains. He asked who he was and what he had done. [34] Some in the crowd were shouting one thing and some another. Since he was not able to get reliable information because of the uproar, he ordered him to be taken into the barracks. [35] When Paul got to the steps, he had to be carried by the soldiers because of the violence of the crowd, [36] for the mass of people followed, yelling, "Get rid of him!"

JOEL 2:28-29

GOD'S PROMISE OF HIS SPIRIT

[28] After this
I will pour out my Spirit on all humanity;
then your sons and your daughters will prophesy,
your old men will have dreams,
and your young men will see visions.
[29] I will even pour out my Spirit
on the male and female slaves in those days.

[13] When Pilate heard these words, he brought Jesus outside. He sat down on the judge's seat in a place called the Stone Pavement (but in Aramaic, Gabbatha). [14] It was the preparation day for the Passover, and it was about noon. Then he told the Jews, "Here is your king!"

[15] They shouted, "Take him away! Take him away! Crucify him!"

Pilate said to them, "Should I crucify your king?"

"We have no king but Caesar!" the chief priests answered.

[16] Then he handed him over to be crucified.

Then they took Jesus away.

RESPONSE

Day 32

What did you notice
about this passage?

What does this teach
you about God?

How does this lead
you to pray?

How are you
challenged to
live differently?

PAUL PREACHES TO JEWS IN JERUSALEM

Day 33

ACTS 21:37-40

PAUL'S DEFENSE BEFORE THE JERUSALEM MOB

³⁷ As he was about to be brought into the barracks, Paul said to the commander, "Am I allowed to say something to you?"

He replied, "You know how to speak Greek? ³⁸ Aren't you the Egyptian who started a revolt some time ago and led four thousand men of the Assassins into the wilderness?"

³⁹ Paul said, "I am a Jewish man from Tarsus of Cilicia, a citizen of an important city. Now I ask you, let me speak to the people."

⁴⁰ After he had given permission, Paul stood on the steps and motioned with his hand to the people. When there was a great hush, he addressed them in Aramaic:

ACTS 22

¹ "Brothers and fathers, listen now to my defense before you." ² When they heard that he was addressing them in Aramaic, they became even

quieter. ³ He continued, "I am a Jew, born in Tarsus of Cilicia but brought up in this city, educated at the feet of Gamaliel according to the law of our ancestors. I was zealous for God, just as all of you are today. ⁴ I persecuted this Way to the death, arresting and putting both men and women in jail, ⁵ as both the high priest and the whole council of elders can testify about me. After I received letters from them to the brothers, I traveled to Damascus to arrest those who were there and bring them to Jerusalem to be punished.

PAUL'S TESTIMONY

⁶ "As I was traveling and approaching Damascus, about noon an intense light from heaven suddenly flashed around me. ⁷ I fell to the ground and heard a voice saying to me, 'Saul, Saul, why are you persecuting me?'

⁸ "I answered, 'Who are you, Lord?'

"He said to me, 'I am Jesus of Nazareth, the one you are persecuting.' ⁹ Now those who were with me saw the light, but they did not hear the voice of the one who was speaking to me.

¹⁰ "I said, 'What should I do, Lord?'

"The Lord told me, 'Get up and go into Damascus, and there you will be told everything that you have been assigned to do.'

¹¹ "Since I couldn't see because of the brightness of the light, I was led by the hand by those who were with me, and went into Damascus. ¹² Someone named Ananias, a devout man according to the law, who had a good reputation with all the Jews living there, ¹³ came and stood by me and said,

'Brother Saul, regain your sight.'

And in that very hour I looked up and saw him. ¹⁴ And he said, 'The God of our ancestors has appointed you to know his will, to see the Righteous One, and to hear the words from his mouth, ¹⁵ since you will be a witness for him to all people of what you have seen and heard. ¹⁶ And now, why are you delaying? Get up and be baptized, and wash away your sins, calling on his name.'

¹⁷ "After I returned to Jerusalem and was praying in the temple, I fell into a trance ¹⁸ and saw him telling me, 'Hurry and get out of Jerusalem

quickly, because they will not accept your testimony about me.'

[19] "But I said, 'Lord, they know that in synagogue after synagogue I had those who believed in you imprisoned and beaten. [20] And when the blood of your witness Stephen was being shed, I stood there giving approval and guarding the clothes of those who killed him.'

[21] "He said to me, 'Go, because I will send you far away to the Gentiles.'"

PAUL'S ROMAN PROTECTION

[22] They listened to him up to this point. Then they raised their voices, shouting, "Wipe this man off the face of the earth! He should not be allowed to live!"

[23] As they were yelling and flinging aside their garments and throwing dust into the air, [24] the commander ordered him to be brought into the barracks, directing that he be interrogated with the scourge to discover the reason they were shouting against him like this. [25] As they stretched him out for the lash, Paul said to the centurion standing by, "Is it legal for you to scourge a man who is a Roman citizen and is uncondemned?"

[26] When the centurion heard this, he went and reported to the commander, saying, "What are you going to do? For this man is a Roman citizen."

[27] The commander came and said to him, "Tell me, are you a Roman citizen?"

"Yes," he said.

[28] The commander replied, "I bought this citizenship for a large amount of money."

"But I was born a citizen," Paul said.

[29] So those who were about to examine him withdrew from him immediately. The commander too was alarmed when he realized Paul was a Roman citizen and he had bound him.

PAUL BEFORE THE SANHEDRIN

[30] The next day, since he wanted to find out exactly why Paul was being accused by the Jews, he released him and instructed the chief priests and all the Sanhedrin to convene. He brought Paul down and placed him before them.

ACTS 23:1-11

[1] Paul looked straight at the Sanhedrin and said, "Brothers, I have lived my life before God in all good conscience to this day." [2] The high priest Ananias ordered those who were standing next to him to strike him on the mouth. [3] Then Paul said to him, "God is going to strike you, you whitewashed wall! You are sitting there judging me according to the law, and yet in violation of the law are you ordering me to be struck?"

[4] Those standing nearby said, "Do you dare revile God's high priest?"

[5] "I did not know, brothers, that he was the high priest," replied Paul. "For it is written, You must not speak evil of a ruler of your people." [6] When Paul realized that one part of them were Sadducees and the other part were Pharisees, he cried out in the Sanhedrin, "Brothers, I am a Pharisee, a son of Pharisees. I am being judged

because of the hope of the resurrection of the dead!" ⁷ When he said this, a dispute broke out between the Pharisees and the Sadducees, and the assembly was divided. ⁸ For the Sadducees say there is no resurrection, and neither angel nor spirit, but the Pharisees affirm them all.

⁹ The shouting grew loud, and some of the scribes of the Pharisees' party got up and argued vehemently: "We find nothing evil in this man. What if a spirit or an angel has spoken to him?"

¹⁰ When the dispute became violent, the commander feared that Paul might be torn apart by them and ordered the troops to go down, take him away from them, and bring him into the barracks. ¹¹ The following night, the Lord stood by him and said, "Have courage! For as you have testified about me in Jerusalem, so it is necessary for you to testify in Rome."

1 PETER 3:21-22

²¹ Baptism, which corresponds to this, now saves you (not as the removal of dirt from the body, but the pledge of a good conscience toward God) through the resurrection of Jesus Christ, ²² who has gone into heaven and is at the right hand of God with angels, authorities, and powers subject to him.

HEBREWS 10:19-22

EXHORTATIONS TO GODLINESS

¹⁹ Therefore, brothers and sisters, since we have boldness to enter the sanctuary through the blood of Jesus— ²⁰ he has inaugurated for us a new and living way through the curtain (that is, through his flesh)— ²¹ and since we have a great high priest over the house of God, ²² let us draw near with a true heart in full assurance of faith, with our hearts sprinkled clean from an evil conscience and our bodies washed in pure water.

RESPONSE

Day 33

What did you notice
about this passage?

What does this teach
you about God?

How does this lead
you to pray?

How are you
challenged to
live differently?

Week 5

THEY ALL JOINED TOGETHER

In the spirit of Acts 2:42, choose a time to gather with a group to read Scripture aloud and discuss the text together. Dig into this passage about the sons of Sceva, and ask that the Holy Spirit would teach you about the character of God from His Word.

TURN TO PAGE 199 AND READ ACTS 19:11–20 TOGETHER. DISCUSS THE PASSAGE USING THE QUESTIONS PROVIDED.

CHECK OUT THE GATHERING GUIDE ON PAGE 136 FOR RECIPE AND HYMN IDEAS TO INCORPORATE INTO YOUR GROUP TIME!

QUESTIONS

1. What do you notice about this passage?

2. Who was working miracles? Who did the sons of Sceva think was making miracles happen? How do you know?

3. Why does reverence for Christ's name matter? How can we use Christ's name?

4. What does this passage teach about those who use the name of Christ for their own benefit instead of His glory?

5. How did God use miracles to magnify His name and further the work of His kingdom?

PRAYER

Close your time together by praying for one another.

GRACE DAY

GRACE DAY

GRACE DAY

GRACE DAY

DAY 34

WEEK 5

GRACE DAY

GRACE DAY

There is no greater prayer we can pray for those we love than for them to know the fullness of God's love in the saving grace of Jesus Christ.

Take this day as an opportunity to catch up on your reading, pray, and rest in the presence of the Lord. Pray Acts 16:31 for a specific person in your life and for yourself.

They said, "Believe in the Lord Jesus, and you will be saved— you and your household."

ACTS 16:31

T
R

U

T
H

Weekly Truth

Memorizing Scripture is one of the best ways to carry God-breathed truth, instruction, and reproof wherever we go.

As we read through Acts, we are memorizing Acts 17:24–29, a passage from Paul's eloquent yet succinct presentation of the gospel to the Greek philosophers at the Areopagus. By memorizing one verse per week, we will have all six verses committed to memory by the end of the study. This week's verse is highlighted here.

²⁴ The God who made the world and everything in it—he is Lord of heaven and earth—does not live in shrines made by hands. ²⁵ Neither is he served by human hands, as though he needed anything, since he himself gives everyone life and breath and all things. ²⁶ From one man he has made every nationality to live over the whole earth and has determined their appointed times and the boundaries of where they live. ²⁷ He did this so that they might seek God, and perhaps they might reach out and find him, though he is not far from each one of us. ²⁸ For in him we live and move and have our being, as even some of your own poets have said, "For we are also his offspring." ²⁹ Since we are God's offspring then, we shouldn't think that the divine nature is like gold or silver or stone, an image fashioned by human art and imagination.

THE PLOT TO KILL PAUL.

Day 36

ACTS 23:12-35

THE PLOT AGAINST PAUL

¹² When it was morning, the Jews formed a conspiracy and bound themselves under a curse not to eat or drink until they had killed Paul. ¹³ There were more than forty who had formed this plot. ¹⁴ These men went to the chief priests and elders and said, "We have bound ourselves under a solemn curse that we won't eat anything until we have killed Paul. ¹⁵ So now you, along with the Sanhedrin, make a request to the commander that he bring him down to you as if you were going to investigate his case more thoroughly. But, before he gets near, we are ready to kill him."

¹⁶ But the son of Paul's sister, hearing about their ambush, came and entered the barracks and reported it to Paul. ¹⁷ Paul called one of the centurions and said, "Take this young man to the commander, because he has something to report to him."

¹⁸ So he took him, brought him to the commander, and said, "The prisoner Paul called me and asked me to bring this young man to you, because he has something to tell you."

¹⁹ The commander took him by the hand, led him aside, and inquired privately, "What is it you have to report to me?"

²⁰ "The Jews," he said, "have agreed to ask you to bring Paul down to the Sanhedrin tomorrow, as though they are going to hold a somewhat more careful inquiry about him. ²¹ Don't let them persuade you, because there are more than forty of them lying in ambush—men who have bound themselves under a curse not to eat or drink until they have killed him. Now they are ready, waiting for your consent."

²² So the commander dismissed the young man and instructed him, "Don't tell anyone that you have informed me about this."

TO CAESAREA BY NIGHT

²³ He summoned two of his centurions and said, "Get two hundred soldiers ready with seventy cavalry and two hundred spearmen to go to Caesarea at nine tonight. ²⁴ Also provide mounts for Paul to ride and bring him safely to Felix the governor."

²⁵ He wrote the following letter:

²⁶ Claudius Lysias,

To the most excellent governor Felix:

Greetings.

²⁷ When this man had been seized by the Jews and was about to be killed by them, I arrived with my troops and rescued him because I learned that he is a Roman citizen. ²⁸ Wanting to know the charge they were accusing him of, I brought him down before their Sanhedrin. ²⁹ I found out that the accusations were concerning questions of their law, and that there was no charge that merited death or imprisonment. ³⁰ When I was informed that there was a plot against the man, I sent him to you right away. I also ordered his accusers to state their case against him in your presence.

³¹ So the soldiers took Paul during the night and brought him to Antipatris as they were ordered. ³² The next day, they returned to the barracks, allowing the cavalry to go on with him. ³³ When these men entered Caesarea and delivered the letter to the governor, they also

presented Paul to him. ³⁴ After he read it, he asked what province he was from. When he learned he was from Cilicia, ³⁵ he said, "I will give you a hearing whenever your accusers also get here." He ordered that he be kept under guard in Herod's palace.

2 CORINTHIANS 4:8–12

⁸ We are afflicted in every way but not crushed; we are perplexed but not in despair; ⁹ we are persecuted but not abandoned; we are struck down but not destroyed. ¹⁰ We always carry the death of Jesus in our body, so that the life of Jesus may also be displayed in our body. ¹¹ For we who live are always being given over to death for Jesus's sake, so that Jesus's life may also be displayed in our mortal flesh. ¹² So then, death is at work in us, but life in you.

JOB 33:4

The Spirit of God has made me,
and the breath of the Almighty gives me life.

RESPONSE

Day 36

What did you notice
about this passage?

What does this teach
you about God?

How does this lead
you to pray?

How are you
challenged to
live differently?

JOURNEY TO ROME

Day 37

ACTS 24

THE ACCUSATION AGAINST PAUL

¹ Five days later Ananias the high priest came down with some elders and a lawyer named Tertullus. These men presented their case against Paul to the governor. ² When Paul was called in, Tertullus began to accuse him and said: "We enjoy great peace because of you, and reforms are taking place for the benefit of this nation because of your foresight. ³ We acknowledge this in every way and everywhere, most excellent Felix, with utmost gratitude. ⁴ But, so that I will not burden you any further, I request that you would be kind enough to give us a brief hearing. ⁵ For we have found this man to be a plague, an agitator among all the Jews throughout the Roman world, and a ringleader of the sect of the Nazarenes. ⁶ He even tried to desecrate the temple, and so we apprehended him. By examining him yourself you will be able to discern the truth about these charges we are bringing against him." ⁹ The Jews also joined in the attack, alleging that these things were true.

PAUL'S DEFENSE BEFORE FELIX

¹⁰ When the governor motioned for him to speak, Paul replied: "Because I know you have been a judge of this nation for many years, I am glad to

offer my defense in what concerns me. [11] You can verify for yourself that it is no more than twelve days since I went up to worship in Jerusalem. [12] They didn't find me arguing with anyone or causing a disturbance among the crowd, either in the temple or in the synagogues or anywhere in the city. [13] Neither can they prove the charges they are now making against me. [14] But I admit this to you: I worship the God of my ancestors according to the Way, which they call a sect, believing everything that is in accordance with the law and written in the prophets. [15] I have a hope in God, which these men themselves also accept, that there will be a resurrection, both of the righteous and the unrighteous. [16] I always strive to have a clear conscience toward God and men. [17] After many years, I came to bring charitable gifts and offerings to my people. [18] While I was doing this, some Jews from Asia found me ritually purified in the temple, without a crowd and without any uproar. [19] It is they who ought to be here before you to bring charges, if they have anything against me. [20] Or let these men here state what wrongdoing they found in me when I stood before the Sanhedrin, [21] other than this one statement I shouted while standing among them, 'Today I am on trial before you concerning the resurrection of the dead.'"

THE VERDICT POSTPONED

[22] Since Felix was well informed about the Way, he adjourned the hearing, saying, "When Lysias the commander comes down, I will decide your case." [23] He ordered that the centurion keep Paul under guard, though he could have some freedom, and that he should not prevent any of his friends from meeting his needs.

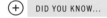 DID YOU KNOW...

While Paul was in prison in Caesarea, the local governor, Felix, and his wife, Drusilla, regularly sent for Paul to listen to him talk about Jesus (Acts 24:24-26).

[24] Several days later, when Felix came with his wife Drusilla, who was Jewish, he sent for Paul and listened to him on the subject of faith in Christ Jesus. [25] Now as he spoke about righteousness, self-control, and the judgment to come, Felix became afraid and replied, "Leave for now, but when I have an opportunity I'll call for you." [26] At the same time he was also hoping that Paul would offer him money. So he sent for him quite often and conversed with him.

[27] After two years had passed, Porcius Festus succeeded Felix, and because Felix wanted to do the Jews a favor, he left Paul in prison.

[10] For this is what the LORD says: "When seventy years for Babylon are complete, I will attend to you and will confirm my promise concerning you to restore you to this place. [11] For I know the plans I have for you"—this is the LORD's declaration—"plans for your well-being, not for disaster, to give you a future and a hope. [12] You will call to me and come and pray to me, and I will listen to you. [13] You will seek me and find me when you search for me with all your heart. [14] I will be found by you"—this is the LORD's declaration—"and I will restore your fortunes and gather you from all the nations and places where I banished you"— this is the LORD's declaration. "I will restore you to the place from which I deported you."

HEBREWS 13:15

Therefore, through him let us continually offer up to God a sacrifice of praise, that is, the fruit of lips that confess his name.

RESPONSE

Day 37

1

What did you notice
about this passage?

2

What does this teach
you about God?

3

How does this lead
you to pray?

4

How are you
challenged to
live differently?

PAUL APPEALS TO CAESAR

Day 38

ACTS 25

APPEAL TO CAESAR

¹ Three days after Festus arrived in the province, he went up to Jerusalem from Caesarea. ² The chief priests and the leaders of the Jews presented their case against Paul to him; and they appealed, ³ asking for a favor against Paul, that Festus summon him to Jerusalem. They were, in fact, preparing an ambush along the road to kill him. ⁴ Festus, however, answered that Paul should be kept at Caesarea, and that he himself was about to go there shortly. ⁵ "Therefore," he said, "let those of you who have authority go down with me and accuse him, if he has done anything wrong."

⁶ When he had spent not more than eight or ten days among them, he went down to Caesarea. The next day, seated at the tribunal, he commanded Paul to be brought in. ⁷ When he arrived, the Jews who had come down from Jerusalem stood around him and brought many serious charges that they were not able to prove. ⁸ Then Paul made his defense: "Neither against the Jewish law, nor against the temple, nor against Caesar have I sinned in any way."

⁹ But Festus, wanting to do the Jews a favor, replied to Paul, "Are you willing to go up to Jerusalem to be tried before me there on these charges?"

¹⁰ Paul replied: "I am standing at Caesar's tribunal, where I ought to be tried. I have done no wrong to the Jews, as even you yourself know very well. ¹¹ If then I did anything wrong and am deserving of death, I am not trying to escape death; but if there is nothing to what these men accuse me of, no one can give me up to them.

I appeal to Caesar!"

¹² Then after Festus conferred with his council, he replied, "You have appealed to Caesar; to Caesar you will go."

KING AGRIPPA AND BERNICE VISIT FESTUS

¹³ Several days later, King Agrippa and Bernice arrived in Caesarea and paid a courtesy call on Festus. ¹⁴ Since they were staying there several days, Festus presented Paul's case to the king, saying, "There's a man who was left as a prisoner by Felix. ¹⁵ When I was in Jerusalem, the chief priests and the elders of the Jews presented their case and asked that he be condemned. ¹⁶ I answered them that it is not the Roman custom to give someone up before the accused faces the accusers and has an opportunity for a defense against the charges. ¹⁷ So when they had assembled here, I did not delay. The next day I took my seat at the tribunal and ordered the man to be brought in. ¹⁸ The accusers stood up but brought no charge against him of the evils I was expecting. ¹⁹ Instead they had some disagreements with him about their own religion and about a certain Jesus, a dead man Paul claimed to be alive. ²⁰ Since I was at a loss in a dispute over such things, I asked him if he wanted to go to Jerusalem and be tried there regarding these matters. ²¹ But when Paul appealed to be held for trial by the Emperor, I ordered him to be kept in custody until I could send him to Caesar."

²² Agrippa said to Festus, "I would like to hear the man myself."

"Tomorrow you will hear him," he replied.

PAUL BEFORE AGRIPPA

²³ So the next day, Agrippa and Bernice came with great pomp and entered the auditorium with the military commanders and prominent

men of the city. When Festus gave the command, Paul was brought in. [24] Then Festus said: "King Agrippa and all men present with us, you see this man. The whole Jewish community has appealed to me concerning him, both in Jerusalem and here, shouting that he should not live any longer. [25] I found that he had not done anything deserving of death, but when he himself appealed to the Emperor, I decided to send him. [26] I have nothing definite to write to my lord about him. Therefore, I have brought him before all of you, and especially before you, King Agrippa, so that after this examination is over, I may have something to write. [27] For it seems unreasonable to me to send a prisoner without indicating the charges against him."

ACTS 26

PAUL'S DEFENSE BEFORE AGRIPPA

[1] Agrippa said to Paul, "You have permission to speak for yourself."

Then Paul stretched out his hand and began his defense: [2] "I consider myself fortunate, that it is before you, King Agrippa, I am to make my defense today against all the accusations of the Jews, [3] especially since you are very knowledgeable about all the Jewish customs and controversies. Therefore I beg you to listen to me patiently.

[4] "All the Jews know my way of life from my youth, which was spent from the beginning among my own people and in Jerusalem. [5] They have known me for a long time, if they are willing to testify, that according to the strictest sect of our religion I lived as a Pharisee. [6] And now I stand on trial because of the hope in what God promised to our ancestors, [7] the promise our twelve tribes hope to reach as they earnestly serve him night and day. King Agrippa, I am being accused by the Jews because of this hope. [8] Why do any of you consider it incredible that God raises the dead? [9] In fact, I myself was convinced that it was necessary to do many things in opposition to the name of Jesus of Nazareth. [10] I actually did this in Jerusalem, and I locked up many of the saints in prison, since I had received authority for that from the chief priests. When they were put to death, I was in agreement against them. [11] In all the synagogues I often punished them and tried to make them blaspheme. Since I was terribly enraged at them, I pursued them even to foreign cities.

[12] "I was traveling to Damascus under these circumstances with authority and a commission from the chief priests. [13] King Agrippa, while on the road at midday, I saw a light from heaven brighter than the sun, shining around me and those traveling with me. [14] We all fell to the ground, and I heard a voice speaking to me in Aramaic, 'Saul, Saul, why are you persecuting me? It is hard for you to kick against the goads.'

[15] "I asked, 'Who are you, Lord?'

"And the Lord replied:

'I am Jesus, the one you are persecuting.

[16] But get up and stand on your feet. For I have appeared to you for this purpose, to appoint you as a servant and a witness of what you have seen and will see of me. [17] I will rescue you from your people and from the Gentiles. I am sending you to them [18] to open their eyes so that they may turn from darkness to light and from the power of Satan to God, that they may receive forgiveness of sins and a share among those who are sanctified by faith in me.'

[19] "So then, King Agrippa, I was not disobedient to the heavenly vision. [20] Instead, I preached to those in Damascus first, and to those in Jerusalem and in all the region of Judea, and to the Gentiles, that they should repent and turn to God, and do works worthy of repentance. [21] For this reason the Jews seized me in the temple and were trying to kill me. [22] To this very day, I have had help from God, and I stand and testify to both small and great, saying nothing other than what the prophets and Moses said would take place— [23] that the Messiah must suffer, and that, as the first to rise from the dead, he would proclaim light to our people and to the Gentiles."

AGRIPPA NOT QUITE PERSUADED

[24] As he was saying these things in his defense, Festus exclaimed in a loud voice, "You're out of your mind, Paul! Too much study is driving you mad."

[25] But Paul replied, "I'm not out of my mind, most excellent Festus. On the contrary, I'm speaking words of truth and good judgment. [26] For the king knows about these matters, and I can speak boldly to him. For I

am convinced that none of these things has escaped his notice, since this was not done in a corner. [27] King Agrippa, do you believe the prophets? I know you believe."

[28] Agrippa said to Paul, "Are you going to persuade me to become a Christian so easily?"

[29] "I wish before God," replied Paul, "that whether easily or with difficulty, not only you but all who listen to me today might become as I am—except for these chains.".

[30] The king, the governor, Bernice, and those sitting with them got up, [31] and when they had left they talked with each other and said, "This man is not doing anything to deserve death or imprisonment."

[32] Agrippa said to Festus, "This man could have been released if he had not appealed to Caesar."

PROVERBS 2:6-8

[6] For the LORD gives wisdom;
from his mouth come knowledge and understanding.
[7] He stores up success for the upright;
He is a shield for those who live with integrity
[8] so that he may guard the paths of justice
and protect the way of his faithful followers.

PSALM 37:28

For the LORD loves justice
and will not abandon his faithful ones.
They are kept safe forever,
but the children of the wicked will be destroyed.

RESPONSE

Day 38

What did you notice
about this passage?

What does this teach
you about God?

How does this lead
you to pray?

How are you
challenged to
live differently?

THE APOSTLES' CREED

Contrary to what its title suggests, the Apostles' Creed was probably not written by Jesus's apostles. Rather, the creed is an early statement of Christian belief in line with what the apostles taught in the New Testament. Today, it serves as a reminder of foundational Christian doctrine for people from a multitude of theological traditions.

1. ROMANS 10:9–10

2. ISAIAH 45:5

3. GENESIS 1–3
   MATTHEW 6:9–13
   JOHN 1:3
   ACTS 14:15

4. MATTHEW 16:13–16
   LUKE 2:11
   JOHN 3:16
   COLOSSIANS 1:15–20

5. LUKE 1:26–37

6. JOHN 18
   LUKE 23:24

7. JOHN 19:20
   ACTS 4:10
   1 CORINTHIANS
   15:3–4

8. 1 CORINTHIANS
   15:42

9. ACTS 1:1–11
   LUKE 24:51
   HEBREWS 1:3

(1) (2) (3)

We believe in God, the Father Almighty,

the Creator of heaven and earth,

(4)

And in Jesus Christ, His only Son, our Lord:

(5)

who was conceived of the Holy Spirit,

born of the virgin Mary,

(6)

suffered under Pontius Pilate,

(7)

was crucified, died, and was buried.

He descended into hell.*

(8)

On the third day He rose again from the dead.

(9)

He ascended into heaven

*The phrase "descended into hell" was added to the creed in the seventh century, and some congregations use a version of the creed without this line.

10. MARK 16:19

(10) and sits at the right hand of God the Father Almighty;

11. MATTHEW 24–25
    2 TIMOTHY 4:1
    JOHN 5:22

(11) from whence He shall come to judge the living and the dead.

12. JOHN 14
    JOHN 15:26
    JOHN 16:7–8, 13

13. MARK 12
    GALATIANS 3:28
    HEBREWS 10:25
    REVELATION 7

(12) We believe in the Holy Spirit, **(13)** the holy catholic** church,

14. MARK 12
    HEBREWS 10:25

15. EXODUS 34
    LUKE 7:48

(14) the communion of saints; **(15)** the forgiveness of sins;

16. 1 THESSALONIANS
    4:16
    ROMANS 8:23
    1CORINTHIANS
    15:51–54

17. JOHN 17:2
    1 CORINTHIANS
    15:42–44

(16) The resurrection of the body; and the **(17)** life everlasting.

18. 2 CORINTHIANS 1:20

(18) *Amen.*

**In the creed, "catholic" means the Church universal; not a specific denomination or location, but all believers over all time.*

PAUL TAKEN TO ROME

Day 39

ACTS 27

SAILING FOR ROME

[1] When it was decided that we were to sail to Italy, they handed over Paul and some other prisoners to a centurion named Julius, of the Imperial Regiment. [2] When we had boarded a ship of Adramyttium, we put to sea, intending to sail to ports along the coast of Asia. Aristarchus, a Macedonian of Thessalonica, was with us. [3] The next day we put in at Sidon, and Julius treated Paul kindly and allowed him to go to his friends to receive their care. [4] When we had put out to sea from there, we sailed along the northern coast of Cyprus because the winds were against us. [5] After sailing through the open sea off Cilicia and Pamphylia, we reached Myra in Lycia. [6] There the centurion found an Alexandrian ship sailing for Italy and put us on board. [7] Sailing slowly for many days, with difficulty we arrived off Cnidus. Since the wind did not allow us to approach it, we sailed along the south side of Crete off Salmone. [8] With still more difficulty we sailed along the coast and came to a place called Fair Havens near the city of Lasea.

PAUL'S ADVICE IGNORED

[9] By now much time had passed, and the voyage was already dangerous. Since the Day of Atonement was already over, Paul gave his advice [10] and

told them, "Men, I can see that this voyage is headed toward disaster and heavy loss, not only of the cargo and the ship but also of our lives." ¹¹ But the centurion paid attention to the captain and the owner of the ship rather than to what Paul said. ¹² Since the harbor was unsuitable to winter in, the majority decided to set sail from there, hoping somehow to reach Phoenix, a harbor on Crete facing the southwest and northwest, and to winter there.

STORM-TOSSED SHIP

¹³ When a gentle south wind sprang up, they thought they had achieved their purpose. They weighed anchor and sailed along the shore of Crete. ¹⁴ But before long, a fierce wind called the "northeaster" rushed down from the island. ¹⁵ Since the ship was caught and unable to head into the wind, we gave way to it and were driven along. ¹⁶ After running under the shelter of a little island called Cauda, we were barely able to get control of the skiff. ¹⁷ After hoisting it up, they used ropes and tackle and girded the ship. Fearing they would run aground on the Syrtis, they lowered the drift-anchor, and in this way they were driven along. ¹⁸ Because we were being severely battered by the storm, they began to jettison the cargo the next day. ¹⁹ On the third day, they threw the ship's tackle overboard with their own hands.

²⁰ For many days neither sun nor stars appeared, and the severe storm kept raging.

Finally all hope was fading that we would be saved.

²¹ Since they had been without food for a long time, Paul then stood up among them and said, "You men should have followed my advice not to sail from Crete and sustain this damage and loss. ²² Now I urge you to take courage, because there will be no loss of any of your lives, but only of the ship. ²³ For last night an angel of the God I belong to and serve stood by me ²⁴ and said, 'Don't be afraid, Paul. It is necessary for you to appear before Caesar. And indeed, God has graciously given you all those who are sailing with you.' ²⁵ So take courage, men, because I believe God that it will be just the way it was told to me. ²⁶ But we have to run aground on some island."

²⁷ When the fourteenth night came, we were drifting in the Adriatic Sea, and about midnight the sailors thought they were approaching land. ²⁸ They took soundings and found it to be a hundred and twenty feet

deep; when they had sailed a little farther and sounded again, they found it to be ninety feet deep. [29] Then, fearing we might run aground on the rocks, they dropped four anchors from the stern and prayed for daylight to come. [30] Some sailors tried to escape from the ship; they had let down the skiff into the sea, pretending that they were going to put out anchors from the bow. [31] Paul said to the centurion and the soldiers, "Unless these men stay in the ship, you cannot be saved." [32] Then the soldiers cut the ropes holding the skiff and let it drop away.

[33] When it was about daylight, Paul urged them all to take food, saying, "Today is the fourteenth day that you have been waiting and going without food, having eaten nothing. [34] So I urge you to take some food. For this is for your survival, since none of you will lose a hair from your head." [35] After he said these things and had taken some bread, he gave thanks to God in the presence of all of them, and after he broke it, he began to eat. [36] They all were encouraged and took food themselves. [37] In all there were 276 of us on the ship. [38] When they had eaten enough, they began to lighten the ship by throwing the grain overboard into the sea.

SHIPWRECK

[39] When daylight came, they did not recognize the land but sighted a bay with a beach. They planned to run the ship ashore if they could. [40] After cutting loose the anchors, they left them in the sea, at the same time loosening the ropes that held the rudders. Then they hoisted the foresail to the wind and headed for the beach. [41] But they struck a sandbar and ran the ship aground. The bow jammed fast and remained immovable, while the stern began to break up by the pounding of the waves. [42] The soldiers' plan was to kill the prisoners so that no one could swim away and escape. [43] But the centurion kept them from carrying out their plan because he wanted to save Paul, and so he ordered those who could swim to jump overboard first and get to land. [44] The rest were to follow, some on planks and some on debris from the ship. In this way, everyone safely reached the shore.

ACTS 28:1-10

MALTA'S HOSPITALITY

[1] Once safely ashore, we then learned that the island was called Malta. [2] The local people showed us extraordinary kindness. They lit a fire and

took us all in, since it was raining and cold. ³ As Paul gathered a bundle of brushwood and put it on the fire, a viper came out because of the heat and fastened itself on his hand. ⁴ When the local people saw the snake hanging from his hand, they said to one another, "This man, no doubt, is a murderer. Even though he has escaped the sea, Justice has not allowed him to live." ⁵ But he shook the snake off into the fire and suffered no harm. ⁶ They expected that he would begin to swell up or suddenly drop dead. After they waited a long time and saw nothing unusual happen to him, they changed their minds and said he was a god.

MINISTRY IN MALTA

⁷ Now in the area around that place was an estate belonging to the leading man of the island, named Publius, who welcomed us and entertained us hospitably for three days. ⁸ Publius's father was in bed suffering from fever and dysentery. Paul went to him, and praying and laying his hands on him, he healed him. ⁹ After this, the rest of those on the island who had diseases also came and were healed. ¹⁰ So they heaped many honors on us, and when we sailed, they gave us what we needed.

LUKE 12:4-7

FEAR GOD

⁴ "I say to you, my friends, don't fear those who kill the body, and after that can do nothing more. ⁵ But I will show you the one to fear: Fear him who has authority to throw people into hell after death. Yes, I say to you, this is the one to fear! ⁶ Aren't five sparrows sold for two pennies? Yet not one of them is forgotten in God's sight. ⁷ Indeed, the hairs of your head are all counted. Don't be afraid; you are worth more than many sparrows."

MARK 16:17-18

¹⁷ "And these signs will accompany those who believe: In my name they will drive out demons; they will speak in new tongues; ¹⁸ they will pick up snakes; if they should drink anything deadly, it will not harm them; they will lay hands on the sick, and they will get well."

RESPONSE

Day 39

What did you notice
about this passage?

What does this teach
you about God?

How does this lead
you to pray?

How are you
challenged to
live differently?

PAUL IN ROME

Day 40

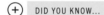 DID YOU KNOW...

Paul spent two years
in Rome under house
arrest. Notable visitors
included Luke (the author
of Acts), John Mark (the
author of the Gospel
of Mark and former
traveling companion
of Paul), Timothy (Paul's
"son in the faith"), and
Onesimus (a runaway
slave who would later
hand deliver Paul's
letters Colossians and
Philemon).

ACTS 28:11-31

ROME AT LAST

¹¹ After three months we set sail in an Alexandrian ship that had wintered at the island, with the Twin Gods as its figurehead. ¹² Putting in at Syracuse, we stayed three days. ¹³ From there, after making a circuit along the coast, we reached Rhegium. After one day a south wind sprang up, and the second day we came to Puteoli. ¹⁴ There we found brothers and sisters and were invited to stay a week with them. And so we came to Rome. ¹⁵ Now the brothers and sisters from there had heard the news about us and had come to meet us as far as the Forum of Appius and the Three Taverns. When Paul saw them, he thanked God and took courage. ¹⁶ When we entered Rome, Paul was allowed to live by himself with the soldier who guarded him.

PAUL'S FIRST INTERVIEW WITH ROMAN JEWS

¹⁷ After three days he called together the leaders of the Jews. When they had gathered he said to them: "Brothers, although I have done nothing against our people or the customs of our ancestors, I was delivered as a prisoner from Jerusalem into the hands of the Romans. ¹⁸ After they examined me, they wanted to release me, since there was no reason for the

death penalty in my case. [19] Because the Jews objected, I was compelled to appeal to Caesar; even though I had no charge to bring against my people. [20] For this reason I've asked to see you and speak to you.

In fact, it is for the hope of Israel that I'm wearing this chain."

[21] Then they said to him, "We haven't received any letters about you from Judea. None of the brothers has come and reported or spoken anything evil about you. [22] But we want to hear what your views are, since we know that people everywhere are speaking against this sect."

THE RESPONSE TO PAUL'S MESSAGE

[23] After arranging a day with him, many came to him at his lodging. From dawn to dusk he expounded and testified about the kingdom of God. He tried to persuade them about Jesus from both the Law of Moses and the Prophets. [24] Some were persuaded by what he said, but others did not believe.

[25] Disagreeing among themselves, they began to leave after Paul made one statement: "The Holy Spirit was right in saying to your ancestors through the prophet Isaiah [26] when he said,

> Go to these people and say:
> You will always be listening,
> but never understanding;
> and you will always be looking,
> but never perceiving.
> [27] For the hearts of these people
> have grown callous,
> their ears are hard of hearing,
> and they have shut their eyes;
> otherwise they might see with their eyes
> and hear with their ears,
> understand with their heart
> and turn,
> and I would heal them.

[28] Therefore, let it be known to you that this salvation of God has been sent to the Gentiles; they will listen."

[30] Paul stayed two whole years in his own rented house. And he welcomed all who visited him, [31] proclaiming the kingdom of God and teaching about the Lord Jesus Christ with all boldness and without hindrance.

ISAIAH 6:9–10

[9] And he replied:

> Go! Say to these people:
> Keep listening, but do not understand;
> keep looking, but do not perceive.
> [10] Make the minds of these people dull;
> deafen their ears and blind their eyes;
> otherwise they might see with their eyes
> and hear with their ears,
> understand with their minds,
> turn back, and be healed.

2 TIMOTHY 4:6–8

[6] For I am already being poured out as a drink offering, and the time for my departure is close. [7] I have fought the good fight, I have finished the race, I have kept the faith. [8] There is reserved for me the crown of righteousness, which the Lord, the righteous Judge, will give me on that day, and not only to me, but to all those who have loved his appearing.

RESPONSE

Day 40

What did you notice
about this passage?

What does this teach
you about God?

How does this lead
you to pray?

How are you
challenged to
live differently?

Week 6

THEY ALL JOINED TOGETHER

In the spirit of Acts 1:14, choose a time to gather with a group to read Scripture aloud and discuss the text together. Consider this account of Paul's time in prison and think about God's work in your own stories. Pray that the Holy Spirit would teach you about the character of God from His Word.

TURN TO PAGE 262 AND READ ACTS 28:23–31 TOGETHER. DISCUSS THE PASSAGE USING THE QUESTIONS PROVIDED.

CHECK OUT THE GATHERING GUIDE ON PAGE 136 FOR RECIPE AND HYMN IDEAS TO INCORPORATE INTO YOUR GROUP TIME!

QUESTIONS

1. What do you notice about this passage?

2. In spite of his imprisonment, Paul was able to receive guests and preach the gospel without impediment. What are some blessings you have experienced in the midst of trial?

3. How much hope did Paul have in earthly justice? What stake do you place in earthly justice?

4. Who did Paul welcome to visit him? How can we also keep our doors open to those who want to learn from us?

5. How does this passage reveal the gracious nature of the gospel?

PRAYER

Close your time together by praying for one another.

GRACE DAY

GRACE DAY

GRACE DAY

GRACE DAY

GRACE DAY

DAY 41

WEEK 6

GRACE DAY

Praise the Lord that the gospel is true!

Take this day as an opportunity to catch up on your reading, pray, and rest in the presence of the Lord. Pray Acts 20:32 for a specific person in your life and for yourself.

And now I commit you to God and to the word of his grace, which is able to build you up and to give you an inheritance among all who are sanctified.

ACTS 20:32

T
R

U

Weekly Truth

Scripture is God-breathed and true. When we memorize it, we carry the gospel with us wherever we go.

As we read through Acts, we have been memorizing Acts 17:24–29, a passage from Paul's eloquent yet succinct presentation of the gospel to the Greek philosophers at the Areopagus. This week we are memorizing the final verse, highlighted here.

T
H

²⁴ The God who made the world and everything in it—he is Lord of heaven and earth—does not live in shrines made by hands. ²⁵ Neither is he served by human hands, as though he needed anything, since he himself gives everyone life and breath and all things. ²⁶ From one man he has made every nationality to live over the whole earth and has determined their appointed times and the boundaries of where they live. ²⁷ He did this so that they might seek God, and perhaps they might reach out and find him, though he is not far from each one of us. ²⁸ For in him we live and move and have our being, as even some of your own poets have said, "For we are also his offspring." ²⁹ Since we are God's offspring then, we shouldn't think that the divine nature is like gold or silver or stone, an image fashioned by human art and imagination.

BENEDICTION

And now I commit you to God and
to the word of his grace, which is able
to build you up and to give you an
inheritance among all who are sanctified.

ACTS 20:32

FOR THE RECORD

(+) WHO DID I STUDY WITH?

(+) WHERE DID WE MEET?

- ○ HOME
- ○ SCHOOL
- ○ OFFICE
- ○ COFFEE SHOP
- ○ CHURCH
- ○ OTHER:

(+) WHEN DID WE MEET?

MONDAY   TUESDAY   WEDNESDAY   THURSDAY   FRIDAY   SATURDAY   SUNDAY

(circle)

- ○ MORNING
- ○ OTHER:
- ○ AFTERNOON
- ○ NIGHT

(+) WHAT WAS I LISTENING TO?

SONG

ARTIST

ALBUM

⊕ WHAT WAS HAPPENING IN MY LIFE?

⊕ WHAT WAS HAPPENING IN THE WORLD?

⊕ TOGETHER, WE PRAYED FOR:

1

2

3

4

END DATE

SHE READS TRUTH ▼ HE READS TRUTH

WOMEN AND MEN IN THE WORD OF GOD EVERY DAY

She Reads Truth and He Reads Truth are communities of women and men who read God's word together every day. We help individuals and groups engage with Scripture through daily Bible reading plans, online essays about each day's reading, and printed resources designed for deeper engagement. Start reading with us today.

@shereadstruth | @hereadstruth | shereadstruth.com | hereadstruth.com

READ TRUTH
WITH US.

Bible reading isn't just for small groups and Sundays—it's for every day in-between! If you're wondering what to read next, we can help. She Reads Truth and He Reads Truth are communities of women and men in the Word of God every day. Simply show up, read today's scriptures with us, and do it again tomorrow. You'll be amazed what a difference regular Bible reading will make.

GRAB A BOOK.

The best all-in experience, our thoughtfully designed books include the full Scripture text for daily readings and theological extras to invite you deeper into God's Word. Study Books (for Shes) and Legacy Books (for Hes) also include dedicated space for you to take notes, record prayers, or reflect on what you've read. View our collection of Study and Legacy Books at ShopSheReadsTruth.com.

DOWNLOAD THE APP.

Whether you're in line for coffee or on your lunch break, the She Reads Truth and He Reads Truth apps bring functional, accessible Bible-reading tools to your fingertips. Each app includes the full text of the Bible in multiple translations, as well as digital reading plans, daily devotionals, customizable reading reminders, and Scripture lock screens for your device. Available on iOS and Android.

RECEIVE DAILY EMAILS.

Sign up to have the daily devotional content from our current reading plan delivered straight to your email inbox each morning. This is a popular option for Shes and Hes who like to read the Scripture text from a Study Book, a Legacy Book, or their Bible.

READ WITH US ONLINE.

Start by reading with us on SheReadsTruth.com and HeReadsTruth.com, which feature the Scripture text and devotionals from both past and present reading plans.

KIDS READ TRUTH

GATHER THE WHOLE FAMILY AROUND GOD'S WORD.

Struggling to find the right resources to introduce the children in your life to the Bible? We've been there, too. That's why our team is committed to creating fun, vibrant, and biblically faithful resources to equip children with biblical literacy and instill in them a love for God's Word.

Discover our collection of storybooks, card sets, art journals, and other products designed for kids, tweens, and families at ShopKidsReadsTruth.com.